THEY NEVER LET A CRISIS GO TO WASTE

Also by Jason Chaffetz

The Deep State: How an Army of Bureaucrats Protected Barack Obama and Is Working to Destroy the Trump Agenda

Power Grab: The Liberal Scheme to Undermine Trump, the GOP, and Our Republic

THEY NEVER LET A
CRISIS
GO TO WASTE

THE TRUTH ABOUT DISASTER LIBERALISM

JASON CHAFFETZ

BROADSIDE BOOKS

An Imprint of HarperCollins*Publishers*

HarperCollins books may be purchased for educational, business, or sales promotional use. For information, please email the Special Markets Department at SPsales@harpercollins.com.

Broadside Books™ and the Broadside logo are trademarks of HarperCollins Publishers.

FIRST EDITION

Library of Congress Cataloging-in-Publication Data has been applied for.

ISBN 978-0-06-306613-7

21 22 23 24 25 LSC 10 9 8 7 6 5 4 3 2 1

Dedicated to:

The People Who Love the United States of America

CONTENTS

INTRODUCTION

As a newly elected member of Congress in 2008, the same election cycle that Barack Obama was elected president, I didn't get to serve with Congressman Rahm Emanuel. He departed to become the incoming White House chief of staff as I was being sworn in for my freshman term. But not long after my first introduction to him, he would make a statement that would come to define the politics of the left throughout the next decade of my political career.

I was new to Congress when Emanuel and I first met. He knew who I was, thanks in part to a cover story by one of the Capitol Hill newspapers profiling me as a freshman who would be sleeping on a cot in my office.

On one of my first trips to Washington, D.C., I had brought with me a cot that I bought at Smith's Food & Drug in Highland, Utah. I hauled it to D.C. wrapped in giant Hefty garbage bags and duct tape. As I rolled off the plane and pulled that duct-taped monstrosity off the baggage carousel, photographers were there waiting to talk to one of the House's newest members. The cot became famous. At least famous enough for the notorious Rahm Emanuel to take notice.

A few weeks later, I met the man known as "Rahmbo" at one of those ubiquitous dinner events for which D.C. is known. As we shook hands his only comment was, "You need to get out of the office more often," with a big smile on his face. Clever. He certainly had his finger, although he is missing one, on the pulse of Washington, D.C., even on a freshman in the minority party.

It wasn't long after I met him that he did a broadcast interview with the *Wall Street Journal* where he was quoted as saying, "You never want a serious crisis to go to waste. And what I mean by that is an opportunity to do things you think you could not do before."

It was a sentiment that reflected a governing philosophy any 2020 election voter can easily recognize—one reflected in the title of this book. I think there was a collective gasp in the Beltway at the time because Emanuel actually articulated what everyone knew to be true. Rahm Emanuel was rooted in politics, partisan to a fault, and as aggressive as they come. Nobody should have been shocked by his comments.

A while later I would learn firsthand the reality of governing by crisis. It is infuriating, frustrating, and wrong. It's why sane people come to the natural conclusion that Washington, D.C., isn't working—driving rational people to the point of disgust.

The question I most often get is, what can I do? How can I make it better? How do I stand up for my family, my community, and my country?

Somehow, some way we have to break the cycle and collectively be brave enough to overcome the impediments to sound public policy. It means flushing out those career politicians who continue to get paid regardless of the outcomes. It means learning to recognize the hypocrisy and hold people accountable for what they do and do not do. It means putting our country before the selfish, petty politics of the moment. It means fighting through the bureaucracy. It means being an adult and having truth-based discussions about the reality of the situation and our future. It also means standing up for our country, our freedoms, our constitution, and understanding our history, the good and the bad, and doing it responsibly in a manner that would make us all proud.

In other words, it is an America First agenda, not just on foreign policy or a particular issue, but in standing up for our country, our flag, our rights, our freedom, and our future. We should learn from the past, strive to become better, respect our neighbors, and love those around us no matter their background.

But in a time of intense polarization, when the overlap between the beliefs of the left and right seems to have disappeared, passing even the most basic legislative solutions has become a heavy lift. To get around this challenge, the left has embraced what I call disaster liberalism.

Disaster liberalism is a means by which Democrats use the threat of an impending crisis to justify enacting unpopular or unconstitutional policies on an accelerated timeline that bypasses traditional checks and balances. Whether the crisis is legitimate, fabricated, or exaggerated, the solution is always the same: more government, less individual freedom, higher spending, higher taxes. Every crisis becomes a vehicle to enact an agenda that could not otherwise gain support in a democratic republic.

This is a strategy that works for the left. Voters tend to trust conservatives on economic policy, individual rights, and foreign policy. But on humanitarian issues, they relate to the emotional appeals of the heart. Disaster liberalism uses that emotional language to attack conservative concerns such as runaway spending, gun rights, or religious liberty as heartless. In this way, they can distract from the power grab buried inside their policy agenda. By cloaking the strengths of conservatism, they also hide the weaknesses of progressivism. But only so long as voters don't catch on. This book is intended to help voters do just that.

I clearly recall my first real taste of disaster liberalism. I had been elected on a promise of reining in government spending. It was my top priority. There was no way I was going to vote for bloated budget bills and opaque earmarks.

Then Hurricane Sandy barreled into the Eastern Seaboard

in 2012, creating a crisis that demanded an expedited response. There would have been real suffering, legitimate need, and dire consequences if we didn't act. Of course I was going to vote in favor of spending to help those devastated by that destructive storm.

But to my disappointment, the so-called emergency spending included $24 billion for line items that wouldn't be spent for at least four years. The emergency response bill included funding for Head Start, new cars for the Drug Enforcement Administration, oil spill research, leaky roofs at the Smithsonian museums, and historic preservation at the National Park Service. The emergency became a vehicle by which pet policy priorities could be funded without the regular order of a budget process. I felt I had no choice but to vote for the bill.

Just like a business or household, when disaster strikes, another part of the budget needs to be adjusted. Heaven forbid we actually budget for contingencies. Though I knew we needed to help those in need, I was frustrated that we didn't have any discussion about where else we could have cut spending for the obvious and deserving disaster funding. Instead we did the opposite. We added new low-priority spending instead of cutting low-priority spending. It was a pattern that would repeat over and over again.

I wrote this book, with my incredibly talented partner in politics for the past decade plus, Jennifer Scott, because I hope people recognize, learn, and never forget what happens time and time again in Washington, D.C. The pandemic of 2020 was perhaps the worst health crisis our nation has experienced in my lifetime. The virus and its wrath was already enough, but far too many in our country used it, the murder of George Floyd, and the presidential election to justify the unjustified.

The pages of this book are intended to give perspective on how liberals use a crisis to further the long-term public policy agenda that they could never achieve through our democratic processes. Many of their goals are truly radical, foreign to our core values, and over-the-top. They have to use a crisis, or create a crisis, to use either a figurative bludgeon or sometimes outright violence, to get their way.

The content of this book will remind you of the perils of progressive policies. These are the same policies they would implement if not for the constant vigilance and effort of the silent majority, the American people. In these times of divided government, understanding these dynamics is more important than ever. When we recognize what they do, how they do it, and why they get away with it, we will all be empowered to fight back for the good of the nation.

THEY NEVER LET A CRISIS GO TO WASTE

CHAPTER I

WHEN THE MASKS CAME OFF

A Watershed Event

In a year of extraordinary events, June 2020 marked an inflection point in American politics. Everything that came after it would be different from what had come before it. Of all the events Americans endured during a year no one wants to replicate, this was the one that changed everything. It was the moment that the COVID pandemic was overturned by more pressing concerns—the political passions of the leftist elite. And we just let it happen. June was when the masks came off and we saw the left for who they really were.

It all started with the murder of George Floyd, which set off nationwide protests that quickly ballooned out of control. The Black Lives Matter protests that month rode a wave of legitimate frustration, harnessing the intensity of a collective rage to power demands for justice. But the anarchists, Antifa, and others who hate America hijacked the outrage and used the protests as an opportunity to destroy communities. If they continue to get their way, the ultimate result will be a new wave of progressive policies. The same kind of policies that have flooded black communities with poverty and crime for decades.

For better or worse, the political aftermath of those protests will likely be seen as a watershed event in American politics—a decade-defining moment that turned the tide of history. But which way will the tide turn? Toward racial harmony, or toward an America stripped of fundamental rights and devoid of the rule of law? Will life return to the normal we once knew, or will a new normal replace it, one that Democrats, liberals, and outright socialists sought to thrust upon us?

These strong tides have a hidden undertow. The peaceful protesters who legitimately demanded racial equality cloaked the more radical and politically motivated efforts to leverage a crisis in the pursuit of power.

I hope there will be a significant upside for those who experience disparate treatment from the criminal justice system in this country. But we can be certain the downside of the protests will be seismic. The hypocrisy these protests exposed has torn the masks off America's elite institutions, exposing their agenda-driven underpinnings that subjugate science to dogma.

COVID-19 was a useful pretext to push progressive policies—until it wasn't. How the Black Lives Matter protests made leftist politicians switch their furor from one crisis to another in an *instant* shows just how politically motivated so many of their actions were. Because of this, the impact of the Black Lives Matter protests will forever be tied to the crisis they upended: a global health pandemic that we were told urgently demanded no one gather—even to protest.

Protests began as a legitimate response to incidents of police brutality and the loss of certain kinds of black lives. The outrage was conveniently selective, only directed at black lives disrupted by police violence, but never at black lives disrupted by criminal or political violence. They became much bigger than simply a civil rights protest, of which there have been many. These protests were distinguished from other civil disobedience in ways both constructive and destructive. The scope of the protests quickly expanded across the country and around the world, drawing attention to certain inexcusable abuses, suppressing others, and shining a spotlight on demands for progressive policies—many with a tenuous link to racism.

Unfortunately, the timing and implementation of the protests sent unintended messages to the American public that led many to question the whole premise of the lockdown. Was it ever really about public health? Or was it political all along? Before the watershed event, the question was a heresy. Afterward, for many, it was a given.

Taking place in the midst of a global pandemic and economic lockdown, the protests' political utility for Democrats was dependent on reversing messaging they had aggressively promoted for weeks. Democrats would attempt to walk it back as time went on, but as May turned to June, the reversal was 180 degrees virtually overnight. The extensive violence, looting, and rioting that characterized the earliest protests—much of it targeting vulnerable black neighborhoods in deep blue cities—contradicted the message that black lives matter. And the selective coverage of the protests sought to emphasize the stories that fit a political narrative while ignoring obvious and egregious counternarrative examples.

Social Distancing? Never Mind

The speed with which America's political, cultural, and media elite reversed their previous messaging on public health in 2020 would give anyone whiplash. The tide turned so quickly from denying free speech and assembly rights in May to demanding them by June that the juxtaposition was jarring. We saw two sets of protests and two sets of standards.

To understand this, we have to go back to the first protests— the ones that took place before June. At first, during the early days of the pandemic, Americans surrendered their rights with surprisingly little pushback. But as the weeks passed and the reality of the lockdown set in, more and more people fought back. During the month of May, in state after state, Americans began to demonstrate against restrictive lockdowns that threatened their livelihoods, their communities, and their way of life. In some cases, the responses were more forceful, with police arresting mothers who let kids play on playgrounds, ticketing churchgoers listening to sermons from their cars, and denying occupational licenses to barbers who opened for business. In states governed by progressive politicians, these protests were met with warnings and reprimands from public health officials and politicians alike. There were heavy doses of public shaming and dire predictions of massive death tolls. In short, the protesters were condemned for putting their civil rights ahead of public safety.

But just weeks and even days later, the much larger and much more violent protests on the left received very different treatment. They weren't condemned by leftist elites, but rather promoted.

This shift was not subtle. It wasn't just the woke scolds on social media whose positions abruptly reversed. It wasn't just the celebrities, or the left-wing newsrooms. It was people with real political power—the blue state politicians who had made shaming protesters part of their agenda and the public health experts who had been peddling fear for weeks.

All of a sudden, social distancing was optional—a mere suggestion to be measured against weightier issues. Overnight, we went from shaming anyone who even questioned public health guidelines to forgetting we even had public health guidelines.

Let's start with the health experts and academics on whose expertise America relied to shut down the economy and destroy many small businesses in the first place. These were the same people warning us in April and May that we should not act too quickly to reopen businesses and leave our homes.

As the riots got under way, I remember thinking to

myself—what are the epidemiologists going to say about this? Given how strongly people had reacted to much smaller protests in Michigan, California, and Wisconsin, what would public health experts, the blue state governors, and the hand-wringing leftist media say now? Would the Party of Science™ tell us the truth when the truth runs against their narrative?

We didn't have to wait long for an answer to those questions. The academics at the University of Washington, whose forecasting model was referenced by federal and state governments to make decisions about the need for lockdowns, were among the first to reverse course.

In a public letter signed by nearly 1,300 health experts from around the country, they highlighted one particular "heavily armed predominantly white" group who was protesting "stay-at-home orders and calls for widespread public masking to prevent the spread of COVID-19." They then went on to broadly sum up the anti-lockdown protests as "white protesters resisting stay-at-home orders." No doubt the many people of color who joined in the lockdown protests across the country were surprised to learn people of their race had been erased from the narrative by these epidemiologists. Furthermore, the reductive description of protests as a tantrum about wearing masks obscured the very real and painful price exacted by the stay-at-home orders. The letter further ignored the many white liberals pushing for less restrictive lockdowns.

Divisions over the economic trade-offs of locking down the economy were hardly racially drawn. Lockdowns also weren't hurting the rich. They took a harder toll on those who were not white-collar workers, on people with smaller houses, bad internet, and no money to stock up on two months of food.

After that inaccurate and wholly incomplete assessment of objections to the lockdown, the public health experts characterized the leftist protests as a "response to ongoing, pervasive, and lethal institutional racism." With that rose-colored description of a weekend that resulted in burned businesses, looted stores, injured protesters, and police, they followed up with, "A public health response to these demonstrations is also warranted, but this message must be wholly different from the response to white protesters resisting stay-at-home orders."

The condescending tone continued with efforts to tie these claims to science. The letter claimed that white supremacy is "a lethal public health issue that predates and contributes to COVID-19" and insisted that "COVID-19 among black patients is yet another lethal manifestation of white supremacy." This is the twisted logic by which a long-standing problem, one apparently not dealt with during the eight years this country was governed by a black president, became so urgent that it could only be dealt with through violent demonstrations in the middle of a global pandemic.

The letter's bottom line was this: "As public health advocates, we do not condemn these gatherings as risky for COVID-19 transmission. . . . This should not be confused with a permissive stance on all gatherings, particularly protests against stay-home orders."

In other words, your protests are not important enough to warrant risking disease transmission. Ours are.

Johns Hopkins epidemiologist Jennifer Nuzzo followed suit, writing on Twitter, "We should always evaluate the risks and benefits of efforts to control the virus. In this moment the public health risks of not protesting to demand an end to systemic racism greatly exceed the harms of the virus."

You know what else rivals the harms of the virus? The risk of cancer patients not seeking treatment, unemployed Americans falling into depression and suicide, or battered women being exposed to increasing levels of domestic violence by their partners who stay home. But none of that mattered before the Black Lives Matter protests. Only after the protests began were we told we were allowed to "evaluate the risks and benefits" of virus-spreading activities. We didn't get to decide whether we believed church services, funerals, or livelihoods were essential—governors decided that for us.

How many Americans died alone in a hospital bed with no visitors to keep the virus from spreading? How many lonely patients in nursing facilities went months without any physical contact with loved ones? How many families were asked to sacrifice the one opportunity to hold or attend a funeral for a parent, grandparent, or child during this time? "Protests against systemic racism, which fosters the disproportionate burden of COVID-19 on Black communities and also perpetuates police violence, must be supported," the letter read.

Here were public health professionals trying to justify why some people could gather by the thousands, shouting, chanting, and in some cases looting and burning, but Americans wanting to end the lockdowns must still stay home.

As inconsistent as some public health officials were from May to June, the politicians were worse. America's most restrictive governors and mayors, who had gleefully used the force of law to prevent women from cutting hair in their homes and kids from playing on playgrounds, were suddenly protesting against law enforcement—marching shoulder to shoulder with thousands of people in violation of their own edicts. The very people upon whom they rely to enforce their broad restrictions—police—were now the enemy.

Illinois governor J. B. Pritzker marched with protesters against police in June. But in May, he was threatening to use those same police to crack down on disobedient businesses. Wallet Hub ranked Pritzker's mandate as the third most strict lockdown in the country. At the time, he emphasized that his plans were "science-based." Where was this science in June?

New Jersey governor Phil Murphy rushed to exempt outdoor gatherings from his restrictive lockdown orders, acknowledging protests needed to be consistent with "the law," aka his edicts (and thus correctly implying they had not been consistent with the law). He did this *after* he had appeared with protesters, violating his own edicts.

Michigan governor Gretchen Whitmer, who had been harshly critical of lockdown protesters who hadn't socially distanced in her state, was photographed marching side by side with a dense crowd of demonstrators. Whitmer justified the photo op because she was wearing a mask—an option she didn't give to churchgoers or small businesses wanting to reopen in her state.

In Seattle, where protesters set up their own Capitol Hill Autonomous Zone (CHAZ) by taking over a police precinct, Mayor Jenny Durkan brushed off the anarchists. She excused the widespread vandalism, violence, and crime as a "block party atmosphere." It was a big shift from her position in 2016, when right-wing Oregon ranchers seized a government wildlife refuge in Oregon. She accused that group, which is believed to have consisted of only a few dozen men, of trashing the place. But when thousands of leftists vandalized public buildings and trashed private businesses, it was a summer of love.

The contradictions were almost too numerous to track. While millions were gathering around the country to protest that black lives matter, it became clear that only certain black lives mattered—those that fit a narrative. Black lives like former police captain David Dorn, who was murdered by looters near St. Louis the night of the riots while protecting a business, got far less attention. Unless you frequent right-leaning media sites, you may have missed it. The lives and livelihoods of poor black families whose neighborhood pharmacies, grocery stores, and fast-food restaurants had been cleared out or set ablaze didn't seem to matter much. Nor those of the black business owners whose life work went up in flames. And certainly not the lives of black people who might be exposed to a deadly disease from which black people were two to three times more likely to die than whites. Unless a black life was taken by a white cop, these lives didn't seem to matter any more than the spread of a deadly pandemic among those most at risk to contract it.

MSNBC's Ali Velshi unwittingly became an internet meme after he stood before a burning building in Minneapolis and reported, "I want to be clear in how I characterize this. This is mostly a protest. It is not, generally speaking, unruly but fires have been started and the crowd is relishing that." Many posted a famous clip of actor Leslie Nielsen in the movie *The Naked Gun* telling bystanders, "Please disperse. Nothing to see here!" as a fireworks warehouse explodes in flames behind him.

In the days that followed, media outlets went out of their way to use the term "peaceful protesters" to describe those attending events in which violent activities had taken place. We were continually reminded that many were wearing masks. We had to learn from Trump administration official Dr. Deborah Birx about the seventy coronavirus testing sites that were destroyed the first weekend of the "peaceful" protests. The media rarely told such stories.

The contrast in the coverage was so obvious, media critic William A. Jacobson told Fox News, "The riots have ripped the mask off the mainstream media-politicized coronavirus hysteria. When it was politically convenient, the media shamed and attacked people who wanted to reopen their stores or even gather at the beach. Now that rioters and looters are gathering in large numbers, the media no longer cares about social distancing, because the media sympathizes with them."

Politico noted the change in tone in a June 4 headline that read, "Suddenly, Public Health Officials Say Social Justice Matters More Than Social Distance." *Politico* cited former Harvard Medical School dean Jeffrey Flier, who said, "Overnight, behaviors seen as dangerous and immoral seemingly became permissible due to a 'greater need.'"

Never-Trumper and *Bulwark* columnist Amanda Carpenter's defense of the Black Lives Matter protests sounded exactly like the arguments that lockdown protesters had been making weeks earlier. She wrote on June 3, "I realize there is lot[s] of scolding of protesters in regards to the pandemic but consider the possibility the protesters think the cause is important enough that they are willing to risk COVID. The situation is dire. Good options are waning." No kidding. Is it possible there may be other issues, in addition to racism, that stir people to protest? To those on the left, prior protests were just a bunch of whiny conservatives worried about their next haircut. No other concerns were recognized.

The double standard on shaming at mass gatherings was widespread. Readers may have read about the lawyer who prowled Florida beaches dressed as the Grim Reaper giving away body bags to beachgoers for failing to stay home during a pandemic. Even he seemed to have changed his tune. By June, his Grim Reaper photos on social media were replaced by photos of his visits to various rallies delivering bottled water.

The same people who days earlier decried the failure to follow Centers for Disease Control and Prevention (CDC) guidelines were falling all over themselves to promote protests that furthered their political agenda, without regard for the warnings they had weaponized against political enemies days earlier.

On social media, where a fierce battle to shame the noncompliant had been raging for weeks, the reversal was easy to document. Historians trying to piece together the hot mess that was 2020 could learn a lot by following the trending hashtags on Twitter, Facebook, and Instagram. Peak shaming was taking place in May 2020. The #Covidiots hashtag was used to call out the sins of people who bought too much toilet paper, hoarded masks, didn't wear masks, gathered with family or friends, wanted haircuts, or questioned the necessity of restrictions. On May 9, one user posted a photo of an April rally at the Wisconsin

Capitol where seventy people later tested positive for COVID-19. The user tweeted,

> LET. EVERY. #COVIDIOT. DIE. GASPING. EVERY ONE of these #COVIDIOTS has WAIVED all right to #COVID treatment. Why endanger health workers treating mass-murderers actively spreading death?

By early June, the same user, who posts under the name Fielding Mellish, was retweeting images encouraging people to show up to protests in multiple cities and repeating conspiracy theories about MAGA voters infiltrating the riots to loot and burn. Gone were the earlier concerns about lockdown protesters as mass murderers actively spreading disease and death.

Other #Covidiot posters deployed a similar double standard. One user pointed the finger at Arkansas churchgoers in May, writing, "What do you have to say about this report today? CDC: 38% of the attendees at an Arkansas church over a week contracted #coronavirus. #covidiots." The same user, a month later, is posting a photo purportedly showing thousands gathered for George Floyd protests in Europe and writing "Thank you #Amsterdam." No #Covidiots called out there.

Another wrote on May 11, "Insisting on your rights without acknowledging your responsibilities isn't freedom, it's adolescence." By June 7, she was posting photos of protests in her own city, writing "I'm very proud."

Perhaps no one has a better story to tell about the shift than *Ricochet* editor and mother of four Bethany Mandel. She is the reason the hashtag #GrandmaKiller began trending on Twitter. In early May, with COVID-19 deaths and hospitalizations falling far short of projections in most states and places like Georgia loosening restrictions, Mandel decried "indefinite lockdowns" and "economic destruction." She mentioned dentists and doctors "going into the red." Mandel had the audacity to express concern for small businesses run by families struggling to meet basic needs. She ended the thread writing, "You can call me a Grandma killer. I'm not sacrificing my home, food on the table, all of our docs and dentists, every form of pleasure (museums, zoos, restaurants), all my kids' teachers in order to make other people comfortable. If you want to stay locked down, do. I'm not."

Left-wing Twitter became apoplectic. Blue-check progressives—verified Twitter accounts with large followings—began retweeting Mandel with pointed critiques. Mandel's tweet almost immediately went viral. The responses were predictably over-the-top.

Former Clinton White House staffer Joe Lockhart replied, "Hi Grandma Killer, Can I also call you Nurse Killer, Friend Killer, Mentor Killer, EMT Killer, Jazz Musician Killer, Doctor Killer, NYPD Killer, Transit Worker Killer, Meat Plant Worker Killer, Immuno-compromised Person Killer? Let me know which works for you."

I went back a month later to see what Joe thought of the Grandma Killers who converged on American cities to "peacefully protest" for Black Lives Matter. One would never know from Lockhart's June Twitter feed that a global pandemic ever happened. This time he expressed no reservations about the potential grandmas, nurses, friends, meat plant workers, or jazz musicians at risk during the Black Lives Matter protests.

Another memorable response read, "Can you imagine being so proud of your anti-social behavior [that] you'd embrace the label 'grandma killer'? That's vice signaling."

By June 1, at the conclusion of the first weekend of Black Lives Matter protests, Mandel discovered that many of those same accounts who had castigated her weeks earlier were now proudly promoting participation in public protests.

One user on May 11 wrote to Mandel, "Here's hoping you and your right wing nuts get the virus bring it home to your own family and friends and not recover. Namaste you stain on humanity. A total disgrace." By June 7, that same user posted a video of a large crowd that was definitely *not* social distancing, commenting on how great it was to see so many show up to protest in the "primarily republican, entitled small town" of Allentown, New Jersey.

June 2020 was a study in contrasts. Moms wanting to take kids to museums in May were Grandma Killers. A month later, looters, arsonists, and rioters were peaceful protesters. All of these heartfelt concerns for the health and safety of the grandmas Bethany Mandel was supposedly killing by taking her kids to a museum or a pediatrician seemed to melt away once the Black Lives Matter protests got under way.

Different Rules for Red States

And then, almost as fast as the tables turned, the winds shifted again. With the announcement in mid-June that President Trump would hold a rally in Tulsa, Oklahoma, mainstream media suddenly remembered there was a virus afoot. The moral authority that the media felt in denouncing COVID ended up melding with their evergreen grievances against the right. Cries for justice—in fact, calls for revenge—ended up being directed right at the people the leftist elites wanted to punish the most.

The contrasting tone and tenor of the news coverage between red state calls to reopen and blue state protests and riots was obvious. When Georgia was the first state to loosen restrictions in late April, the headline in *The Atlantic* read, "Georgia's Experiment in Human Sacrifice: The state is about to find out how many people need to lose their lives to shore up the economy." The answer: very few. Case counts in Georgia remained consistent in the weeks following the late April reopening, only surging again in late June, weeks after the Black Lives Matter riots.

To its credit, *The Atlantic* actually did cover the potential public health impact of the Black Lives Matter protests as they were happening, albeit with a lot less hyperbole than the Georgia headline. Their June 1 story ran with the more benign headline, "The Protests Will Spread the Coronavirus" and provided numerous justifications for public protesting during a pandemic. It explained why resulting outbreaks would likely be the fault of police for using tear gas, funneling people into smaller spaces, and putting looters in cramped jails where the disease can more easily spread.

In another story from *The Atlantic*, epidemiologists Julia Marcus of Harvard and Gregg Gonsalves of Yale tried to clean up the mess that public health officials had made of their own credibility. In a June 11 piece titled "Public Health Experts Are Not Hypocrites" they kept digging the hole deeper. "Supporting one kind of protest but not another may seem confusing at first," they wrote, "but the decision reflects what public-health experts have always tried to do: Maximize the health of the population across all aspects of life. And health is about more than simply remaining free of coronavirus infection." Except that wasn't what public health experts had always tried to do. Refer back to the open letter from 1,300 epidemiologists that both Marcus and Gonsalves had signed. Anyone who questioned whether economic lockdowns might be a cure worse than the disease was labeled a white supremacist protester.

The epidemiologists went on. "The anti-lockdown demonstrations were explicitly at odds with public health, and experts had a duty to oppose them. The current protests, in contrast, are a grassroots uprising against systemic racism, a pervasive and long-standing public-health crisis that leads to more than 80,000 excess deaths among black Americans every year." As if lockdown impacts like suicide, domestic violence, or forgoing cancer screenings and treatments are not also long-standing public health crises.

The View's Joy Behar tried to justify the Black Lives Matter riots and simultaneously condemn the Trump rally. She told viewers the Trump rally would be a "ten times worse" health risk than the Black Lives Matter protest. "The rally for Trump is indoors," the comedian said. "The protesters are out in the streets and most of them are wearing masks, I notice, even though a lot of them are not. And they should be, but the indoor situation is ten times worse and much more dangerous. That's all. It's completely different."

When I went back six weeks after the protests to find out what impact they had on the spread of the virus, I was inundated with spin. Though case counts had proliferated, left-wing media was tying itself into knots to make sure the public knew the protests had nothing to do with it. By contrast, coverage of the Trump rally in Tulsa was very definitive, amplifying speculation of a local COVID spike related to the rally. The differences in the coverage were stark.

The Colorado Sun on June 30 ran with this headline: "Black Lives Matter Protests May Have Slowed Overall Spread of Coronavirus in Denver and Other Cities, New Study Finds." Authors concluded that fewer people got the virus because they were staying home to avoid the protests. Nevertheless, case counts steadily climbed following the protests. Colorado saw a steady rise in cases beginning June 14—two weeks after the protests.

More data is needed to determine the exact causes of the summer spike in cases that swept the nation. It may be that the protests directly spread the virus. But it's also possible the protests sent a message to the nation that the lockdowns were over—that contact tracing was now impossible and spread could not possibly be contained.

The takeaway for conservatives after the June riots could be summed up in a June 6 Twitter thread from *Resurgent* columnist Drew Holden:

> Seriously, if Dems pull a full about-face on quarantine, it'll validate every person who ever said that something like electing Trump needed to happen. Conservatives played by the rules.

And then the Dems changed them the moment it suited them. The media, our society's watchdogs, golf-clapped along, and republicans got screwed for doing the right thing.

It will be an inescapable proof positive that it's not possible to just win on the policy, or play by the rules, or be nice. It'll be a [reification] that politics is a blood sport and nice guys lose. That you need, first [and] foremost, a fighter, everything else is secondary.

It'll show that the left has carte blanche to restrict your liberty, to destroy your business, to keep you from your loved ones, to suffocate your freedom, and then flip the switch when it no longer suits them. And that no force in society can or will hold them accountable. So if this happens, I don't want to hear it. I don't want the debates. I don't want the Lincoln Project selfimolating [*sic*] bullshit. Not another word of it.

When the masks came off, the truth became clear: the lockdowns weren't just about public health. They also became a pretext to move forward a political agenda. They were intended to lead to a new normal—an America more easily controlled by a government less easily constrained. Who knew Make America Great Again would actually become a reference to the halcyon days of 2019? The fight would be about returning to the unprecedented freedom and prosperity of the early Trump years.

The Black Lives Matter protests weren't just about racism. They were a pretext for promoting a Marxist agenda—a war with the rule of law. Nothing moves an agenda forward like a good crisis—as long as politicians don't let the crisis go to waste.

CHAPTER 2

THE "PUBLIC HEALTH CRISIS" PLAYBOOK

If ever there was an event that met the definition of a public health crisis, the global pandemic of 2020 qualified. One early model from the Imperial College of London simulated a projection of 2.2 million deaths in the United States alone, assuming no change in behavior. The left, however, sensing an opportunity, quickly used the crisis to promote their preferred policies, turning unrelated issues into "essential" elements in fighting the pandemic. They did what they always do—used euphemized language to mask cynical power grabs, used kids and the vulnerable as political leverage, and attacked the Constitution.

That's not to say the crisis wasn't real. In fact, even as experts were scrambling to provide reliable advice, ordinary Americans understood on a gut level that something was wrong, and many—uncertain what else to do—swarmed grocery stores and hoarded essentials at the beginning of the pandemic. In the earliest stages, reporting out of China created reasonable fear here at home. We saw efforts to build a Chinese hospital in a week. There were ominous warnings from Chinese health providers suggesting the numbers were much higher than reported. Men in hazmat suits inexplicably sprayed aerosol on the streets. We heard reports of people being sealed into their apartments in forced quarantines and cities being locked down. Varying degrees of panic set in. The natural urge to protect ourselves and our loved ones from a coming threat led to widespread support for President Trump's voluntary "15 days to stop the spread" initiative.

What our political leaders and even our medical experts initially told us turned out to be fundamentally wrong. Amid the growing fear, Speaker Nancy Pelosi urged people to come to Chinatown; New York City mayor Bill de Blasio rode the subway and kept it open; New York governor Andrew Cuomo required infected patients to return to nursing homes; and the U.S. surgeon general, Jerome Adams, warned against wearing masks.

The threat created a degree of anxiety and panic that opened the door for a forceful government response. The left quickly figured out how conveniently they could leverage the crisis to grow the government. They called for a top-down government plan, a reliance on experts to dictate behavior, and the temporary suspension of certain rights and liberties in order to stop the spread. Though such measures have long been viewed in this country with suspicion, the nature of the pandemic created a permissive atmosphere for broad government action in the face of an unpredictable threat.

In this divided nation, a growing contingency on the left already holds near-religious faith in the power of government to heal society's ills. They believe the best way to solve problems is by concentrating more power at the federal level, where uniform solutions can be imposed by "experts" who know what is best for each of us. They are comfortable deferring to professionals and bureaucrats rather than markets or individuals. They seek experts to plan their economies and communities. They support policies that empower others to make decisions about who provides our health care, how we're allowed to defend our homes from crime, how we should spend our discretionary income, and what types of speech we're allowed to express or post to social media. They have no qualms about trimming back some of the broad constitutional protections to which Americans are entitled. The emergence of a true public health crisis created perfect conditions for moving the country toward the big-government solutions the left so eagerly sought to pursue.

Ironically, as the left was happily seeking to force government into our lives in even more ways, they were accusing Donald J. Trump of being an authoritarian. He showed no interest in playing the role. Trump was no fan of the one-size-fits-all, leftist-expert-driven federal solution to all problems. He steadfastly refused to impose a uniform solution across the entire nation. He didn't trust international or government organizations to be completely driven by science and free of political influence.

Leftists Have Done This Before

The utility of a public health crisis for advancing leftist political views is not a recent discovery. Leftists have applied the term "public health crisis" to a wide range of social ills in an effort to create a sense of urgency and promote the types of solutions they favor. In 2020, this strategy went into overdrive.

Despite the serious public health crisis that reared its head in 2020, Americans were still inundated with messaging about other public health crises—racism, gun violence, climate change, access to "reproductive health" (abortion). All of it was a crisis, and all of it demanded the same solution: more government.

As Ryan McMaken, senior editor at the Mises Institute, observed, " 'Public health crisis' is essentially a left-wing stock phrase at this point." McMaken noted that gun violence is now branded as a "public health crisis," as are poverty, inequality, traffic deaths, inadequate housing, and capitalism. There's a reason for that. McMaken wrote,

> In an age of supercharged state institutions, public health is far more characterized by laws, regulations, coercion, punishment, and mandatory "compliance." The very use of the phrase "'public health crisis" is designed to justify these measures. After all, if something is a threat to public health, we must surely all agree it is of the utmost importance. The Left has mastered the use of this phrase as a political ploy. "Public health," after all is just a matter of scientific objectivity, and those who disagree are "anti-science." It's a very effective ruse. It remains to be seen how long people will fall for it.

Indeed, each of these public health crises has been accompanied by appeals to authority, calls to grow government, demands to restrict freedom, and efforts to impose one-size-fits-all solutions on every community (in other words, authoritarianism). One major way in which the left smuggles radical ideas into public parlance is by using euphemisms for hard-sell policies. Politics is filled with words and phrases that mean something completely different than the literal definition of the individual words. Some are euphemisms, like "women's health" as a code word for the process by which women end the lives of their unborn babies in the womb. Others are scary words misapplied to describe political adversaries. Words like "Nazi" or "fascist" when used to describe anyone on the right, "xenophobe" when applied to someone who believes in enforcing national borders, or "hate speech" when used to describe differing opinions. Sometimes the words are actual antonyms that mean the opposite of their literal definition. For example, "Planned Parenthood"—an organization whose primary goal is to prevent parenthood and provides no actual parental planning. Or labeling as racist those who oppose the consideration of race in admissions, hiring, or government aid programs.

This strategy of co-opting language has long been used by lawmakers across the political spectrum to make their policies seem more appealing. Think of the "Affordable Care Act," which by design was not affordable. Studies have shown the Obama health care law actually increased health care premiums (by 62 percent, according to the 2018 Health Insurance Price Index Report). The program was many things, but affordable was never one of them. Or the 2020 Equality Act, passed by House Democrats to single out people and organizations with traditional beliefs about gender and human sexuality for disparate and punitive treatment. Later in this work, we'll look at Nancy Pelosi's "HEROES Act," a name that implied the act gave assistance to teachers and medical providers during a pandemic. In truth, the act was really a vehicle to pass unpopular left-wing spending priorities with the barest connection to the public health crisis.

In our English language, words have a denotation—a literal meaning—and a connotation—what they mean in a certain context. To understand how politicians have leveraged current crises for political advantage, one must understand the way words have been manipulated to create the appearance of consensus. The best example from 2020 of a phrase that has taken on a different meaning is "black lives matter"—a sentiment with which few Americans would take issue. All people are created equal. There is an organization using the name, but the media portrays it as a civil rights group committed to peaceful protest. It's more than that.

Black Lives Matter (the proper noun) isn't just a sentiment or a movement to equalize the status of black people—even if that's how it is portrayed. In reality, the Black Lives Matter Global Network is a foundation with a website. At the time the protests were taking place the group had a written manifesto on its "What We Believe" page that outlined a far-left political agenda. According to that page, the group's priorities include dismantling "cisgender privilege" and uplifting "trans gender black folk, especially Black trans women." Whatever one's views of transgender policy issues, they are not the policies people believe they are supporting when they think of the term "black lives matter."

The page also commits to dismantle the patriarchy and "disrupt the Western-prescribed nuclear family structure." Though statistical and scientific evidence strongly supports the outcomes of children raised in nuclear families, this group's agenda is to disrupt that support system and replace it with alternatives that empirically hurt black communities. The group further calls for a national defunding of police that will disproportionately impact the security and stability of impoverished minority neighborhoods. Then they call for "investment in our communities," by which they mean government investment that redistributes wealth and incentivizes government dependency. They do not mean private investment, church investment, or charter school investment that might actually help empower people in black communities. They mean taxpayer subsidies—otherwise known as free stuff.

Entire books could be written on this topic, but suffice it to say, when you embrace the Black Lives Matter slogan, you are also promoting a set of solutions—perhaps unknowingly.

What is their solution to the public health crisis called racism? "Defund the police," they tell us. But don't think for one minute that this is a call for a spending cut. It never is. In a June *New York Times* op-ed titled "Yes, We Mean Literally Abolish the Police," Mariame Kaba, who is billed as an "organizer against criminalization," explains what defund the police actually means: "We should redirect the billions that now go to police departments toward providing health care, housing, education and good jobs. If we did this, there would be less need for the police in the first place."

Not surprisingly, the movement to defund police is just another way of growing government. Police departments' funding would become yet another source of revenue to feed a ravenous leftist agenda. Instead of funding law and order, that money would be spent to grow government. And not just any kind of government—federal government, the most expensive kind. Federal policies come with extensive regulatory compliance, personnel costs, and high barriers to reform. It takes an act of Congress to change them and an act of the judiciary to hold accountable anyone who abuses them. Unlike the private sector, the federal public sector can't easily fire an employee for incompetence.

Every government redistribution program comes with extensive overhead costs—salaries and bricks and mortar that eat up large chunks of the money. Some of the water may eventually reach the end of the row, but not before Democratic constituencies ranging from federal bureaucrats to government contractors to left-leaning nonprofits and progressive academia all get their cut. Redirecting money away from police, which is largely governed and funded at the local level, to federal programs places government in the very lucrative role of middleman. Federal employees would stand between what people earn and what they spend those earnings on and between what they pay in taxes and where those tax dollars end up. Tax dollars currently collected or distributed at the local level would be redirected to federally dictated health care, housing, and education programs.

The same strategy has been used with regard to climate change—an uncontroversial concept in a world that has been changing for millennia. But when one supports the climate change agenda, one is not just agreeing that the climate changes, or even that humans are impacting the climate. Supporting climate change means advocating for policy solutions that dramatically increase energy regulation and cost—solutions that are not backed by science, have no empirical success, and will be wildly disruptive to our economic well-being and political stability.

California's rolling blackouts in the summers of 2019 and 2020 are a testament to the triumph of hope over science, as the state's commitment to renewable energy could not overcome the scientific reality of base-load power supply. The fact is, only fossil-fuel-generated and nuclear power can sustain the kind of consistent power generation needed to keep the lights on during hot, dark, windless summer nights. But the left isn't interested in those types of power sources, science or no science.

The Left's One-Size-Fits-All Solution: More Government

The pandemic once again showed us how the left's solution to every crisis is more government, more spending, more control over our decisions and our incomes. It is a testament to leftist commitment to these principles that they were willing to overcome their deranged hatred of Donald Trump enough to demand he play the role of authoritarian in those crises.

The left demanded uniformity in solutions—a federal mandate regulating the behavior of every American, determining which businesses and activities are essential, who should wear masks and when, and even which widely available medicines doctors are allowed to prescribe. For the first time in American history, they wanted the federal government (not state or local) to be able to arbitrarily dictate whether and under what conditions we could protest, go to church, operate a business, patronize a business, recreate outdoors, or educate our kids. The left was incensed by President Trump's unwillingness to usurp such power and to in some cases let those decisions be made by governments closer to the people.

In addition to massive regulatory power, the left also used the public health crisis to advocate for expansive new spending programs. Once again, Medicare-for-All was presented as a panacea for health care. Medicare-for-All would replace hundreds of thousands of private sector jobs with new taxpayer-funded institutions governed by politicians. What could go wrong? NBC's Michelle Chan explained the argument: "A global health threat requires a maximally inclusive medical infrastructure that can comprehensively manage risks across the population." It seems to me that the term "maximally inclusive" is just another way of saying one-size-fits-all. Like so many leftist policies, this solution relies on a massive transfer of assets and wealth out of the private sector and into the politician-controlled public sector.

In early March, *Vice* published a story with this subheadline: "One thing you can do about coronavirus? Vote for the candidate who is most likely to make universal health care a reality." It urged that the "threat of coronavirus only makes the case for universal policies like Bernie Sanders' signature Medicare-for-All more urgent."

I see two problems with the argument that the COVID-19 crisis makes government expansion urgent. First, the unintended consequences of bad policies become more broadly distributed when applied universally. Second, universal policies rarely live up to their billing. What they can do in theory is always more impressive than what they actually do in practice. They unerringly deliver on the bigger government, bigger spending parts, but fail to deliver the effective solutions they promise. As those on the right recognize, *bigger government is rarely better government.*

With regard to the first problem, let's imagine if the COVID-19 policies of blue state governors had been universal. For example, the states that mandated nursing homes take back contagious

patients. What would the disease progression have looked like
had Governor Cuomo's original policy of forcing long-term care
facilities to accept COVID-19-positive patients been a one-size-
fits-all proposition imposed across the entire country by a powerful federal government? What would it have taken to reverse
it? The bigger the government, the more difficult it is to steer, to
make adjustments, or to reverse course.

What if lengthy and restrictive lockdowns like those in New
York, Michigan, and California had been forced on every state,
regardless of its exposure to the virus? The economic impact of
such a move would have been catastrophic—even by 2020 standards. Meanwhile the public health benefit of lockdowns, even
months after the fact, is still unclear. When the virus made a
second wave during the summer of 2020, it hit lockdown states
like California and open states like Georgia alike. An analysis
by analytics firm TrendMacro concluded that locking down the
economy didn't contain the spread of disease and reopening did
not unleash a wave of infections. In a September 2, 2020, *Wall
Street Journal* piece, TrendMacro chief investment officer Donald Luskin wrote, "Lockdowns were an expensive treatment
with serious side effects and no benefit to society." To date, there
is little evidence to suggest states with long restrictive lockdowns
had any better results than states that quickly reopened.

But the bigger challenge is the gap between what leftists
claim their policies will achieve and what they actually achieve.
Proponents of big-government solutions will often appeal to the
power of expertise, looking to professors, researchers, and other
scholars who can theoretically make better decisions for our lives
than we can. The crisis is the perfect excuse. Wouldn't an epidemiologist know better than we do how to respond? Except many
epidemiologists changed their guidance based on their political
biases when the nature of the protests suited them. Many on the
left urged people to go out and protest with Black Lives Matter

even as they condemned protests against the lockdowns as a public health risk.

The difference between theory and practice can clearly be seen in the public health fiasco that was Obamacare. It wasn't that long ago that we were being promised the so-called Affordable Care Act would cut premiums by $2,500 a year, allow us to choose our doctors and hospitals, and insure more people. None of that came to pass. The tax increases came to pass. The growth in government certainly happened. But for those who pay for their own premiums, costs rose dramatically. People lost their doctors and their choice of hospitals. Employer-provided health plans increasingly came with large deductibles and higher out-of-pocket costs. The individual market virtually disappeared, taking with it slimmer and more affordable plan options that became illegal under Obamacare. The law insured different people, not necessarily more people, as the self-employed and low-income workers got priced out of the insurance market. Though more of the very poor were able to get subsidized insurance, that coverage came at the expense of the self-employed and working poor, who made too much to receive subsidies and too little to pay the five-figure deductibles on top of sky-high premiums. Working Americans discovered they were now expected to cover their own health care and that of the ever-increasing subsidized population.

Whether the crisis is racism, climate change, or public health, the solutions don't change: more government control over the economy and the individual are always the go-to answers. Solutions generally fall into two categories—they either dramatically increase federal spending or they dramatically increase federal regulatory power. Often both. Either way, the outcome is the same: power that is more concentrated and less dispersed. Power surrendered from individuals to "experts" or to a government increasingly controlled by the powerful and the elite; a big government predominantly staffed by leftists, influenced exclusively by a few heavily populated municipal areas, and hostile to the values of Americans outside those leftist enclaves. Leftist ideology seeks more power to control our decisions, our income, and our votes. It demands a more authoritarian system. The crisis is the pretext by which the real goal is achieved.

Using Kids for Political Leverage

Among the demands made by the United Teachers Los Angeles union in exchange for their members agreeing to return to the classroom for the 2020–2021 school year were some big asks. Before they would concede to do the job they were paid to do, they literally demanded an act of Congress. More than one, as a matter of fact.

Their return to the classroom would be conditional upon Congress passing the HEROES Act—a relief bill written by Democrats and designed to enrich key Democratic constituencies, including wealthy taxpayers in blue states. We'll take a closer look at that bill later in this book, but suffice it to say it provided a half-trillion-dollar bailout from the federal government to state and local governments as well as K–12 schools. The union further demanded a massive new entitlement—Medicare-for-All—a plan then–Vice President Joe Biden said in a February 7, 2020, presidential debate would "cost more than the entire federal budget that we spend now." That policy was such a heavy lift that even with a Democratic president, the House, and a sixty-vote majority in the Senate in 2009, Democrats couldn't make it happen, opting instead for a scaled-back version known as Obamacare, which was disastrous enough. But now teachers were demanding it as a condition of returning to work in the fall of 2020.

The union went on to demand a moratorium on private schools at a time when demand for their services was peaking.

They called for defunding of the police. The language of a research paper accompanying the demands was blatantly political. It demanded that California's "record number of millionaires and billionaires finally pay their fair share." This in a state that is already subject to extreme budget volatility from its precarious dependence on a relatively small number of high earners.

Other teachers' unions followed suit. In Durham, North Carolina—a blue island in a traditionally red state—the Durham Association of Educators made similar demands. They called for the implementation of the Democrats' national agenda before they felt safe going back to school. That included socialized medicine, redistribution of income to illegal immigrant families, moratoriums on rent and mortgages, and a complete statewide economic lockdown. The union acknowledged that "all children are suffering without school—some without enough food to eat, others without sufficiently supportive adult and peer relationships, many without internet access, and others with too much mindless screen time." But political priorities were more important to the teachers of Durham, North Carolina.

With weeks to go before schools were slated to reopen in many states, unions found themselves in a position of leverage. Kids were suffering. They were falling behind. They had been stuck at home for months with limited access to outdoor recreation. Special needs students had not been receiving needed services since March. In some places the economy had never reopened. Businesses were struggling to stay afloat. Parents needed to get back to work. Childcare was hard to come by.

Some teachers' unions saw just one thing: leverage. They could leverage the suffering of kids, the struggling economy, and the desperation of state and local leaders to do something important. How did they choose to use that leverage? The crises change, but for leftists, the solutions are always the same. More money. More regulation. More power. More control.

The editorial board at the *Wall Street Journal* summed it up nicely.

> By now you may be getting the idea that the union really doesn't want its members to return to work. Or they're using the pandemic as leverage to extort more money from taxpayers that they couldn't get otherwise. Either way it's a demonstration of how far left the nation's public unions have moved. They're still a self-serving guild, but they're also a political vanguard for left-wing ideological causes. Show them the money, or students can stay home and lose another year of learning.

Welcome to disaster liberalism at its worst. Once again, the crisis is just the pretext by which the real goal is achieved.

The Greatest Obstacle to Progressive Policies: The Constitution

What stands in the way of the real goal? What prevents the quest for a more authoritarian America in which a strong central government can carry out the whims of the left unimpeded? Nothing less than the Constitution of the United States of America.

With its individual rights, separations of powers, and checks and balances, that document has become inconvenient to power mongers and naïve dreamers alike. It prevents the left from concentrating enough power to carry out the most ambitious items on its agenda. That was the trade-off to which the Founding Fathers agreed. In exchange for protection against tyranny, we would accept the high cost and inefficiency of a democratic republic.

Witness the tweet from former Obama administration aide Dan Pfeiffer in July 2020. He wrote, chafing against one of the Constitution's more potent checks and balances, "The Supreme Court is the greatest obstacle to progressive policies in America. . . . Court expansion is the thing we have to do." I enjoyed the response from *National Review*'s David Harsanyi: "In other words," he replied, "the Constitution is the obstacle to authoritarianism." And aren't we thankful that it is?

Those guaranteed natural rights and structural supports inscribed therein demand a system that is expensive, inefficient, and decentralized at the federal level. That is the price of freedom. After all, one Fidel Castro is much cheaper than 535 elected members of the House and Senate, a separate judiciary, and fifty separate state governments. We could do everything so much faster and cheaper if we were willing to entrust the whole mechanism to one person! Having a single leader dictate policy is much more efficient than trying to build consensus among a diverse population. Granted, the left is not advocating for a dictatorship. But their arguments are indistinguishable from those a would-be dictator would make. They are certainly chafing against the limitations put in place by America's Founders.

Imposing one-size-fits-all solutions across the nation is easier than dealing with a patchwork of states using different rules. The Founders knew this. And they thought freedom and liberty were worth the price. Because they knew that concentrated power never remains benign. Power corrupts, nineteenth-century British politician Lord Acton famously opined. But absolute power corrupts absolutely.

History is on the side of the Founders. We can argue about definitions of socialism, communism, Nazism, and every other disastrous system of government. But there is one reality that can't be disputed. Freedom begets prosperity and stability. It always has. It always will. This is truth.

The recognition of these truths is a big part of what drives modern conservatism. No doubt progressives in academia, where Marxist thought is prevalent, are doing their worst to produce studies challenging these conclusions. It's an important debate that I encourage readers to research. Many great books have been written conclusively affirming the efficacy of these values. But for most of us who align with the right, these facts are not in dispute. I believe, ultimately, freedom has already proven to be the right side of history. Individuals, not experts, should be the ones making decisions about their own lives.

During the Obama administration, the term "right side of history" was frequently used to refer to the administration's proposals, while the policy proposals of conservatives were depicted as "the wrong side of history." Conservative commentator Ben Shapiro wrote a masterful book using history, philosophy, and reality to thoroughly refute the administration's thesis. But to this day, the left clings to failed policies like Obamacare, failed ideologies like Marxism, and failed leaders like Joe Biden to declare them the "right side of history." They claim the mantle of the "Party of Science" to buttress their view that more of our decisions should be outsourced to a government full of experts.

Authoritarianism—whatever form it takes—has never been able to hold a candle to the results freedom can produce. Governments that continually restrict individual freedom are less productive, offer lower standards of living, and suffer much wider gaps between rich and poor. For all the excesses of capitalism, the flaws of democracy, and the downsides of free markets, the proof is in the outcomes. The Bible tells us "By their fruits ye shall know them." America has borne her fruit. And it is the envy of the world.

CHAPTER 3

THE PARTY OF SCIENCE?

The month of April 2020 was a deadly time to be a long-term-care patient in the state of New York. With coronavirus raging and skilled nursing facilities packed, Governor Cuomo in late March ordered nursing homes to accept COVID-19 patients. The death toll in these facilities, where the highest concentration of high-risk patients lived in proximity, predictably surged. It's hard to tell by how much. The state of New York steadfastly refused to provide complete numbers in the months following the surge, insisting that New York ranked forty-sixth out of fifty states in the proportion of COVID-19 fatalities who are nursing home patients. But official state tallies didn't square with the number of deaths reported at care homes—a fact the *New York Post* pointed out as early as May 2.

By May 5, the New York State Department of Health had updated its number of deaths to show that 4,800 nursing home patients had died, adding 1,700 people who were never tested, despite showing classic symptoms of COVID-19. And that was just the beginning.

Though nursing homes in New York are required to report

mortality figures in daily filings that include both on-site and off-site deaths, the state only released the numbers for on-site deaths. Even a Freedom of Information Act (FOIA) request and a subsequent lawsuit by the Empire Center for Public Policy has not, as of this writing, shaken loose that data, which is likely to be damning. Empire Center's Bill Hammond estimates the actual toll may be over ten thousand nursing home deaths—about 10 percent of that state's total nursing home population. The Kaiser Family Foundation estimates more than eleven thousand could have died in nursing homes if New York were assumed to have the same percentage of nursing home deaths as the forty-three other states who have provided data.

Ironically, the thousands of nursing home deaths reported on May 5 came at a time in which thousands of New York–area overflow hospital beds were closed. By all accounts, New York–area nursing homes were experiencing a crisis.

New York–area hospitals apparently were not. As patients were dying in nursing homes unprepared to fight COVID, temporary field hospitals were closing after having seen little use. They included a four-thousand-bed field hospital in the Javits Convention Center, the one-thousand-bed U.S. naval ship *Comfort*, and a sixty-eight-ICU-bed field hospital in Central Park operated by Christian charity Samaritan's Purse. Other field hospitals constructed by the Army Corps of Engineers, which spent $350 million building and outfitting overflow hospitals, never even opened.

The USNS *Comfort*, which had entered New York Harbor with great fanfare on March 30, left just over a month later having served just 182 patients. Even as nursing homes were overrun, the *Comfort* was underutilized. As the deadly month of April came to a close, Governor Cuomo told President Trump the ship wasn't needed. "I said we don't really need the *Comfort* anymore. It did give us comfort, but we don't need it anymore, so if they need to deploy it somewhere else, they should take it," Cuomo said on MSNBC's *Deadline: White House.*

The Javits Center likewise saw few patients. Though the facility could handle 2,500 at one time, it ultimately treated just under 1,100 in the total time it was open. Meanwhile, the hospital set up inside New York City's Central Park was practically chased out of town. Run by a Christian charity founded by evangelist Franklin Graham, the fourteen-tent Samaritan's Purse field hospital relieved the overflow of patients from New York's Mount Sinai hospitals. Without cost to the people of New York, the charity operated from April 1 to May 5—a time when the virus was spreading unchecked through nursing homes in the greater New York area. Though the hospital's sixty-eight-bed unit treated more than three hundred patients, some New Yorkers treated the hospital with hostility over its religious roots. The hospital's lifesaving mission was dismissed in light of Graham's rejection of gay marriage and abortion—beliefs leftists embrace with religious zeal.

On May 1, as deaths in New York nursing homes were spiking and nursing home administrators were begging for help, New York City Council Speaker Corey Johnson set straight the city's real priorities. "It is time for Samaritan's Purse to leave NYC," he tweeted on May 1. "This group, led by the notoriously bigoted, hate-spewing Franklin Graham, came at a time when our city couldn't in good conscience turn away any offer of help. That time has passed. Their continued presence here is an affront to our values of inclusion, and is painful for all New Yorkers who care deeply about the LGBTQ community." It would have been nice, had dying nursing home patients been such an affront to their values. Instead, they would demonstrate the value of inclusion by exclusion.

Meanwhile, just twelve days earlier, four members of the New York City Council pleaded for help on behalf of nursing homes. Mark Treyger led three other council members in writing a letter to Mayor Bill de Blasio and Governor Cuomo asking them to allow nursing homes to send contagious patients to the heavily underutilized Javits Center.

"We are getting reports of war zones in nursing homes without adequate doctors, PPE, cleaning supplies, and tests," they wrote. "It is our responsibility to create safe spaces for our seniors as they are being ravaged by this disease in their homes and in medical facilities." The letter then proposed a plan to transport infected nursing home patients "to empty beds at Javits and US *Comfort* and other federal field hospitals to get adequate and safe care."

I don't know whether it was a good plan, but at least it was a plan. But two weeks later, all of those facilities were shuttered.

It wasn't as if no one told the state what was happening. Earlier in April, nursing homes had begun sounding the alarm. One nursing home CEO sent an email to city health officials, according to reporting by the *New York Post*. The Cobble Hill Health Center in Brooklyn had lost fifty-five patients to COVID-19 when CEO Donny Tuchman sent an April 9 email asking if there was "a way for us to send our suspected covid patients" to the convention center or the USNS *Comfort*. At the time, the Javits Center had 1,000 beds completed and just 134 patients, according to the *Post*'s reporting.

The request was denied. "I was told those facilities were only for hospitals" to send their overflow patients, Tuchman said. Incidentally, hospitals in New York are a powerful and deep-pocketed interest group that have given generously to Governor Cuomo's campaign.

Coincidentally, the same day New York announced the jaw-dropping 4,800 nursing home deaths, the *Washington Post* published a fawning homage to New York governor Andrew Cuomo by Never Trump columnist Jennifer Rubin.

Rubin fangirled over Cuomo's remarks at a press conference earlier in the week in which he explained his approach. You have to act with "the best information you have, learning from the lessons you have . . . which means, don't act emotionally," Cuomo had said. In a not-so-subtle jab at President Trump, Cuomo had added: "Don't act because 'I feel this, I feel that.' . . . Forget the anecdotal, forget the atmospheric, forget the environmental, forget the emotional. Look at the data. Look at the measurements. Look at the science. Follow the facts."

Rubin lauded Cuomo's supposedly science-driven approach, writing, "That is as good a model of government decision-making as you will hear, and a complete repudiation of the unscientific (or anti-scientific), impulsive style of political theater now in vogue with many Republicans."

At that very moment, New York nursing homes were drowning in contagious COVID-19 patients. In direct contradiction of guidance from the Centers for Medicare & Medicaid Services (CMS), in contradiction of guidance from scientific experts— denying "the science," if you will—Cuomo had issued his order mandating that nursing homes accommodate infected patients. Other blue state governors had impulsively followed suit. Meanwhile, Republican-led Florida, with little fanfare or, as Rubin would call it, "political theater," was following guidance from CMS and seeing a fraction of the nursing home deaths.

But Rubin, praising Cuomo's approach to reopening the state's economy, noted, "Thousands of lives hang in the balance depending upon how elected leaders make their decisions. Trump operates without data (Liberate Michigan!). New York . . . does the opposite."

But did it do the opposite? Apparently not. The guidance from Trump-appointed CMS administrator Seema Verma was issued March 13. It very specifically and definitively warned that "under no circumstances should a hospital discharge a patient to a nursing home that is not prepared to take care of those patients' needs."

It doesn't take a scientist to understand why that guidance

was given. For some reason, blue state governors—who according to Rubin definitely do not "govern from the gut"—rejected the guidance of big-government public health experts they normally extol.

Just twelve days after the CMS guidance was given, Cuomo's Department of Health would issue his order mandating that "no resident shall be denied re-admission or admission to the [nursing home] solely based on a confirmed or suspected diagnosis of Covid-19." The order also banned facilities from testing new patients before admitting them.

The decision proved lethal for thousands of nursing home staff and patients in New York. A database maintained by the *New York Times* counted more than 28,000 deaths among nursing home residents and staff by mid-June. At the time, that number was one-third of all COVID-19 deaths in America. By late June, nursing home deaths around the country would make up nearly half of all fatalities.

Cuomo wasn't alone. Pennsylvania issued a similar order on March 18—just six days after the CMS guidance was given. New Jersey did the same on March 31 and Michigan followed on April 15. California enacted the policy on March 30, but fortunately rescinded it days later. Ultimately twelve states issued such orders, although some were more careful to ensure COVID patients were never in the same facilities with non-COVID patients.

Confronted with early reports of nursing home infections connected to his order, Cuomo was defiant, criticizing facilities who objected to the order. "They don't have a right to object," he said in an April 23 news conference. "That is the rule and that is the regulation, and they have to comply with that. If they can't do it, we'll put them in a facility that can do it."

So much for science.

The Society for Post-Acute and Long-Term Care Medicine took issue with Cuomo's approach. "We find the New York state advisory to be over-reaching, not consistent with science, unenforceable, and beyond all, not in the least consistent with patient safety principles," the organization said in a statement.

Asked about Tuchman's request to send nursing home patients to field hospitals, Cuomo suggested the nursing home just didn't want to lose money by formally requesting a transfer to a hospital. "Ohh, money," the governor mocked during his April 27 press conference. He blamed federal protocols that he said prevented federal facilities from taking patients from nursing homes. Still, he did not rescind his order.

It wasn't until May 10, after the field hospitals were gone and thousands had already died, that Cuomo finally rescinded the mandate for nursing homes to take COVID patients. By early July, with more than 6,400 New York nursing home residents dead and many more uncounted who were transferred and died in hospitals, Cuomo blamed infected nursing home staff for the disease spread and pointed the finger at President Trump.

In a briefing, Cuomo said, "The president says a lot of things. He makes up facts. He makes up science. He wants to deny the COVID virus; he has since day one. Now we have a problem in thirty-eight states because some people believed him."

In this case, the science was not on Cuomo's side. It was Cuomo and his fellow blue state governors who denied the science, making them the real Grandma Killers.

Cuomo wasn't alone in making disastrous medical decisions for his state. In a September 2020 *USA Today* editorial, Michigan physician assistant Jordan Warnsholz described the fatal outcomes of Governor Gretchen Whitmer's extended ban on elective medical procedures and surgeries in her state—a move Warnsholz said showed "a shocking ignorance of how medicine works." Warnsholz, who is suing the governor for violating the state's constitution by claiming emergency powers beyond the twenty-eight-day period allowed by law, described multiple cases in which patients suffered long-term harm while awaiting elective surgeries. In one case a woman nearly lost her leg awaiting a simple procedure to improve blood flow to it. In another case, he described a diabetic patient whose foot had to be amputated and who days later died after he was unable to get regular treatment because of Whitmer's order.

The Politics of Science

All politicians like to appeal to science to legitimize their ideas. But Democrats in particular have gone to great lengths to brand their party as the Party of Science. Some on social media have taken to sarcastically adding a trademark symbol after the phrase, indicating that it has become a sort of unofficial party slogan. The Party of Science likes to believe their decisions are rational, not political; legitimate, not emotional; based in replicable and incontrovertible science. In their world, science always points to a need for a strong central government with broad powers (controlled by the Party of Science™, naturally).

In a floor speech before the House of Representatives on June 26, Speaker Nancy Pelosi exemplified this line of reasoning, saying of Republicans, "They do not accept science. And they do not accept governance. Wear a mask, wash your hands, keep your distance, they don't want any of that."

It was a silly remark. Science—the scientific messaging put out by experts—was the reason so many people were confused about masks in the first place. On January 31, the CDC advised, "CDC does not currently recommend the use of face masks for the general public. . . . We don't routinely recommend the use of face masks by the public to prevent respiratory illness and certainly are not recommending that at this time for this new virus." The advice was reiterated in subsequent briefings through March 10. U.S. surgeon general Jerome Adams advised on March 31 that "the data doesn't show" that wearing masks in public would prevent disease transmission, which *was* true. Some data was promising, but hardly conclusive at the time.

In those early days, the country did not yet suspect the virus might be spreading through asymptomatic carriers. As that theory became accepted, guidance changed—not based on politics, but on science. We still didn't have incontrovertible data on mask use, but given the very real threat of asymptomatic spread, it became the least restrictive tool in our arsenal and a reasonable alternative to halting economic activity. Early data suggests masks probably do help reduce spread, but more definitive answers await further studies.

On April 3 the CDC revised its guidance on masks. Surgeon General Adams also followed suit, urging Americans to embrace more freedom to go out by wearing a mask.

As for Pelosi's claims that Republicans reject hand washing and social distancing, she would be hard-pressed to find a quote from any prominent or nonprominent Republican opposing those practices. Her argument was little more than a straw man. But this is the way the Party of Science™ wields science as a weapon. It's more of a rhetorical device than a true policy guide. It's helpful to promote crises that propel the progressive agenda—like climate change. But when science gets in the way of that agenda—as when it can't identify more than two genders, can't sustain consistent power generation using only renewable sources, or demonstrates the very human traits of an unborn fetus—science is rejected by the left.

For all of Pelosi's claims about the administration rejecting the science regarding community spread, which they clearly did not, she herself was on the record urging people to avoid social distancing at the earliest stages of infection, when it mattered most. After all, nearly a full month after President Trump closed U.S. borders to China to prevent the spread, Pelosi on February 24 was inviting people to "come to Chinatown. Precautions have been taken. . . . We think it's very safe and want others to come."

This came on the heels of leftist politicians and media outlets rejecting Trump's quick action to cut off travel from disease-ridden China. Some three million people are estimated to travel from China to the U.S. annually, which averages 250,000 people per month, or 8,300 per day according to a *Breitbart* analysis.

But in a House hearing on February 5, House Foreign Affairs Committee chairman Eliot L. Engel, Democrat of New York, panned the decision. "The United States and other countries around the world have put in place unprecedented travel restrictions in response to the virus," he said. "These measures have not proven to improve public health outcomes, rather they tend to cause economic harm and to stoke racist and discriminatory responses to this epidemic." Apparently it's okay to consider the economic harm from lockdowns when China is the country being harmed.

Leftist news outlets were quick to fight science with "science" following Trump's travel restrictions.

BuzzFeed News cited "experts" who criticized the measure as an "overreach." Global health law expert Lawrence Gostin of Georgetown University explained that "barring foreign travelers from China, along with making U.S. citizens self-quarantine at home . . . likely violated civil rights laws, without leading to any real lowered risk of a U.S. outbreak." The *Washington Post* cited "public health experts" who warned that "the move could do more harm than good." If you didn't know better, you might think these were quotations from lockdown protesters in Michigan or Wisconsin—the ones Democrats would later castigate for protesting.

Laurie Garrett at *Foreign Policy* pointed to praise of China's response from WHO director-general Tedros Adhanom, who had said, "China is actually setting a new standard for outbreak response." This as the virus was traveling around the world infecting civilians on six continents. Garrett then opined:

> The epidemic control efforts unfolding today in China— including placing some 100 million citizens on lockdown, shutting down a national holiday, building enormous quarantine hospitals in days' time, and ramping up 24-hour manufacturing of medical equipment—indeed are gargantuan. It's impossible to watch them without wondering, "What would we do? How would my government respond if this virus spread across my country?"

The day after President Trump announced the travel restrictions on China, presidential candidate Joe Biden tweeted, "We are in the midst of a crisis with the coronavirus. We need to lead the way with science—not Donald Trump's record of hysteria, xenophobia, and fear-mongering. He is the worst possible person to lead our country through a global health emergency."

Biden's comments, coming as they did on the heels of the China closure, were widely interpreted to be a reference to the China travel ban. President Trump cited the tweet repeatedly. As the efficacy of Trump's decision became clearer, Biden's team clarified the tweet, saying it did not explicitly tie xenophobia to the travel restriction. PolitiFact dismissed the tweet as merely one in a series of Biden calling Trump xenophobic and hysterical as part of his stump speech, rather than as a specific response to the travel ban.

Whatever Biden's intent, Trump's decision would land on the right side of history. That Biden's team later distanced him from the popular interpretation of his tweet is indicative of that.

Dr. Anthony Fauci would ultimately testify before House lawmakers that the decision was the right one, that it saved lives, and that he was actively involved in making it.

Despite the heavy criticism in the U.S. of the China and subsequent travel bans, other countries around the world, particularly in Europe, began to close their own borders to travelers from China. By early May, the *New York Times* reported, "At least 93 percent of the global population now lives in countries with coronavirus-related travel restrictions."

Eventually, even the Party of Science™ would come around to the idea that travel restrictions were necessary. They would never admit Trump was right. This is how *Vox* admitted they were wrong about Trump's travel ban. On March 24, the *Vox* account tweeted, "We have deleted a tweet from Jan 31 that no longer reflects the current reality of the coronavirus story." That was it. It didn't clarify that the tweet in question linked to their story criticizing Trump's travel ban. The tweet had been headlined, "Is it going to be a deadly pandemic? No."

Instead of acknowledging the wisdom of the travel ban, many on the left reversed their position, memory-holed their own opposition to the ban, and criticized Trump for waiting too long to impose the restrictions or for allowing expatriates living in China to return home. It seemed whatever position was most helpful to Democrats in the upcoming presidential election was the position "public health experts" were taking.

No wonder Americans were so confused by the conflicting guidance from experts. Public health experts were about to become the weapon of choice in the presidential election campaign of 2020.

The Politicized Opposition to Hydroxychloroquine

Perhaps the most egregious example of politics driving science is the suppression of a promising and inexpensive drug treatment for COVID-19. The drug, hydroxychloroquine (HCQ), became the object of an unprecedented national public relations campaign to discredit the treatment before science could even weigh in. Despite promising trials in China and France, the response to the drug in the U.S. turned hostile after President Trump expressed early optimism about its use.

HCQ is an antimalarial treatment that is also routinely used by lupus and arthritis patients. The drug was approved for medical use in the U.S. in 1955 and has been safely used ever since. During a March 13, 2020, coronavirus task force briefing, President Trump enthusiastically touted HCQ as a potential "game changer" against COVID-19. Six days later he announced the Food and Drug Administration (FDA) would fast-track approval of the drug for treatment of COVID-19 patients following promising results from doctors in the U.S., Europe, and China. The next day, Trump made the mistake of praising the drug publicly during a presidential election year, thus inadvertently ensuring the left would go all-in to discredit the treatment. "We ought to give it a try. I feel good about it," Trump said. The reference to his feelings ignited a firestorm of indignation.

From that point forward, the Party of Science™ was fully invested in the failure of the drug. Academia, public health officials, pundits, and politicians all seemed to be rooting against the drug's success. Governors began dictating how doctors could do their jobs. Twitter, Facebook, and YouTube suppressed what they called "misleading" information about the drug—which often comprised opinions of medical professionals who had used the drug and reported positive results.

Having been in the crosshairs of the medical marijuana debate more than once during my time in Congress, I have to wonder how many marijuana proponents would be comfortable applying this standard to information about that drug. I can't count how many times I've been told large-scale medical marijuana studies were insufficient or flawed. Yet proponents persevere.

It wasn't just a question of whether the drug worked. There was an active campaign to convince the world it would kill us. During the first wave of disease progression in the United States, doctors were discouraged from using the treatment in the earliest stages—during the time proponents argued it was most effective. In New York, for example, Governor Cuomo ordered HCQ prescriptions be restricted to those COVID patients in clinical trials, which essentially restricted it to those with already advanced illness. In other states, doctors were legally prevented from prescribing the drug to anyone outside of a hospital setting. Clinical trials were designed to test the drug's efficacy only in the late stages. Given the claims of frontline doctors who had reported developing successful protocols, this effort to withhold the drug until late in the disease cycle would ensure its failure. Some believed that was by design. Either way, the impact was the same: it created fodder for prematurely discrediting the treatment.

Two days after Trump expressed hope about the drug, Wanda Lenius and her husband, Gary, became sick in Arizona after drinking a fish tank cleaner with the word "chloroquine" in the ingredient list. Gary died thirty minutes after ingesting the chemical. Meanwhile, Wanda told the media they had ingested the cleaner after watching President Trump's press conference. She said she looked at the cleaner she used for her koi fish habitat and thought, "Hey, isn't that the stuff they're talking about on TV?"

The story went viral. Left-leaning media uncritically repeated the preposterous story, never questioning whether someone would logically believe fish tank cleaner was a safe medication.

One month later, after the damage was done, the real truth began to spill out—though it didn't go viral in the same way. In reality, the caricature of Wanda Lenius as some uneducated redneck Trump supporter scrupulously following the advice of her president was wrong.

According to reporting by the *Washington Free Beacon*, she was actually a Democrat donor who has given thousands of dollars to Democratic-aligned groups and candidates, including Hillary Clinton. In late February, she donated to a Democratic PAC called the 314 Action Fund, which had been on the front lines of criticizing Trump's coronavirus response.

It gets crazier. The PAC to which she donated is part of the "pro-science resistance." It claims to be "the largest pro-science advocacy organization committed to electing scientists" and aims to "promote the responsible use of data driven fact-based approaches in public policy."

The Party of Science™, at your service. The incident was a tragic one, but one that was probably caused by individual hysteria.

Political Suppression of a Possible Treatment

Whether or not the drug works as a cure or a treatment is one question. But whether or not medical doctors should be able to talk about it, study it, or prescribe it is quite another. Neither question should be driven by politics. But discussions about them were.

As physicians began prescribing HCQ, both as a treatment and a prophylactic to prevent COVID-19, politicians took notice.

One in five prescriptions in this country involve a drug that is prescribed for off-label use—in other words, used to treat a different condition than one for which it was approved. Off-label use of safe and effective drugs is common. But in a fraught political environment, it suddenly became perilous.

On March 25, Nevada Democratic governor Steve Sisolak signed an emergency regulation arbitrarily restricting doctors from treating COVID-19 patients with HCQ outside of an emergency room or hospital setting. That order ensured patients would only get the drug during the latest stages, when doctors who have used it say it is least effective. Numerous subsequent studies, including one from the U.S. Department of Veterans Affairs (VA) in which the drug was administered late in the disease progression, found it had little impact at that late stage. But that was the only stage at which Sisolak would allow the drug to be administered.

Democratic governors found other ways to restrict the drug's use. In Michigan and New York, COVID-19 sufferers were banned from being treated with the drug at all. In Minnesota, Governor Tim Walz signed an executive order authorizing the Minnesota Board of Pharmacy to restrict prescriptions to thirty days and only with "an appropriate diagnosis." What other FDA-approved, widely used drug has ever inspired this level of interference from the political class? Do we really want to live in a country where our access to medical treatments is dictated not by our need or by the advice of our physician, but by the impact of that treatment on the next election? Do we want content moderators at YouTube deciding what information we're allowed to consume about potential treatments?

Stoking fear of the drug, the *Washington Post* in July cited a Brazilian study of the related drug chloroquine that had been discontinued after eleven patients died from the treatment. The story failed to mention that patients had been given lethal cumulative doses of the drug.

With a strong track record of safety, promising testimonials from doctors and patients, and the potential for easy access for patients of all income levels, this is a drug one might assume we would want to thoroughly research and test before disregarding its potential as a treatment. But instead, there was a rush to discredit the drug before proper trials could even be completed. The FDA specifically warned against using HCQ at the early stage, going so far as to revoke emergency approval of the drug as a treatment for COVID-19 in June, long before conclusive results were available. That's important because Oxford University researchers later discovered that it's likely only to be effective in the early stage.

Though the federal government had millions of doses of the drug donated to the Strategic National Stockpile, the FDA would not allow those doses to be used for COVID-19 patients. Medical and pharmacy boards in both red and blue states threatened disciplinary action against providers who dispensed the drug for early treatment or prevention. In England, doctors acknowledged in August 2020 that future studies of the drug were being scrapped because of "intense politization and negativity." Researchers told the BBC a global Oxford University study of forty thousand frontline workers was in jeopardy because the controversy surrounding the drug was making it difficult to recruit participants.

A federal right-to-try law signed by President Trump in 2018 protects the rights of terminally ill patients to try potentially life-saving experimental treatments. Similar laws have been passed with strong support in forty-one states. Though such laws don't apply to FDA-approved treatments like HCQ, we know there is widespread public support for giving patients the option to try potentially lifesaving drugs.

Nevertheless, the left seemed invested in discarding the drug before science could get a chance to conclusively weigh in. When Trump tweeted about a promising study in the *International*

Journal of Antimicrobial Agents, public health experts criticized the study's methodology. When the *Wall Street Journal* published an editorial about the promising treatment, the *New York Times* ran a story (later debunked) alleging Trump had financial ties to Sanofi, the manufacturer of the drug.

In mid-May, the *Washington Post* had published a scary article implying the drug would kill people, with a headline claiming HCQ was "increasingly linked to deaths." Quoting President Trump's challenge to try the drug—"What the hell do you have to lose?"—the article answered, "Growing evidence shows that, for many, the answer is their lives." The evidence-free takes lit up the internet. *NowThis News* called HCQ "potentially lethal." Celebrity Barbra Streisand tweeted that HCQ "could be deadly when misused." (Incidentally, so can ibuprofen and Tylenol.)

The back-and-forth continued. The American Association of Physicians and Surgeons (AAPS) released a statement suggesting HCQ had a 90 percent chance of helping patients. Then the prestigious journal *The Lancet* published a study showing the drug led to a higher risk of heart disease and death.

MSNBC helpfully promoted the *Lancet* study, tweeting, "Hydroxychloroquine, the antimalarial drug touted by President Trump, is linked to increased risk of death in coronavirus patients, according to analysis of 96,000 patients published in the *Lancet*. Hydroxychloroquine is unproven for treating coronavirus." They weren't the only one. The press gleefully saturated the airwaves with stories based on the *Lancet* study.

That study, published on May 22, had to be retracted by June 4. It turns out the data upon which it was based could not be verified as valid by an independent third-party review. But the damage was done.

Virologist Steven Hatfill of George Washington University Medical Center described what happened next:

Continuing patient enrollment needed for early-use clinical trials of hydroxychloroquine dried up within a week. Patients were afraid to take the drug, doctors became afraid to prescribe it, pharmacies refused to fill prescriptions, and in a rush of incompetent analysis and non-existent senior leadership, the FDA revoked its Emergency Use Authorization for the drug.

A backlash to the scaremongering developed online, where patients who had taken the drug for decades questioned the claims about heart damage.

On May 18, President Trump admitted he had been using HCQ himself, setting off another round of inexplicable fury on the left. The war of the studies continued. Public health agencies from the WHO to the CDC to the National Institutes of Health (NIH) all panned the drug, discontinuing ongoing trials or discouraging doctors from using the treatment. When in early June a large government-funded clinical trial in the United Kingdom determined HCQ did not reduce the risk of death among hospitalized patients, *Stat* reported the study would possibly close the door on the use of the drug. Of course, like so many studies at the time, that study relied on using the drug late in the disease progression, after patients had already been hospitalized.

The Oxford University researchers acknowledged the problem with previous studies. "We know now that it doesn't work in treatment of hospitalised patients," Professor Nick White, one of the Oxford study's investigators, told the BBC in early August. "But it still is a medicine that may prove beneficial in preventing Covid-19." Whether it would or wouldn't, we should want to know the answer definitively one way or the other. But many didn't want to know. They just wanted the drug discredited.

The AAPS, a right-leaning physician and surgeon group, alleged in mid-June that previous studies were suspect, writing,

"How can we trust the established authorities or prestigious journals when, in this perilous time, trials of an available, inexpensive, long-established drug appear to be designed to fail, while risking the lives of their subjects through deliberate or negligent drug overdoses?" U.S. media largely ignored the AAPS's concerns, perhaps turned off by the fact that the group's general counsel is none other than Andrew Schlafly, son of Eagle Forum founder Phyllis Schlafly.

Nevertheless, doctors around the world were continuing to have success with the drug. In early July, a major observational study of early intervention with the drug was finally released. Henry Ford Health found HCQ administered early to 2,571 patients across its six hospitals "significantly" decreased death rates and did not result in heart-related side effects. "We attribute our findings that differ from other studies to early treatment, and part of a combination of interventions that were done in supportive care of patients, including careful cardiac monitoring," said Dr. Marcus Zervos, division head of infectious disease for the health system.

This book is not a medical journal, nor do I have a crystal ball to tell me what the outlook for HCQ will be by the time this book gets into readers' hands. As of this writing, some people believe the drug has been discredited and others still assert the drug appears promising when used at the appropriate time and with appropriate treatments. New studies are encountering barriers due to the intense negativity surrounding the drug, so it may be some time before we get answers—if we ever get them.

Nevertheless, the long-term risk of using a safe drug that may not work has to be weighed against the long-term impact of allowing politicians to tell doctors which FDA-approved drugs they are allowed to prescribe to patients. That was the most disturbing part of the HCQ controversy.

None of this was normal. It wasn't indicative of a party driven by science. It was a political game with lives at stake.

When Science Doesn't Fit the Narrative

If the science on mask wearing, border closing, and drug treatments wasn't enough to confuse Americans, "the science" behind public gatherings has to take the cake for most confusing and contradictory. From a public health perspective, it didn't make a lot of sense. Only when you view it from a political perspective—with an eye to how each decision might impact an election—does it begin to make sense. Somehow it was only ever right-wingers or states with Republican governors that were the problem.

Earlier we looked at the public health experts' opinion on protests—they were okay if they were protesting racism, but deadly if they were protesting lockdowns. Being outside in large groups to protest racism was okay as long as you were wearing a mask. But being outside on a beach, socially distanced, was not okay.

Remember Daniel Uhlfelder, the lawyer in the Grim Reaper costume who haunted Florida beaches to shame beachgoers in May? The one who gleefully posted photos of himself delivering bottled water to outdoor Black Lives Matter protesters in multiple cities? We might have expected his beach visits to conclude once the cat was out of the bag on his double standard. But we would have been wrong. Uhlfelder, who is suing Florida governor Ron DeSantis for opening Florida beaches prematurely, was back at it again by July, roaming beaches with his giant scythe to let vacationers know that unlike Black Lives Matters protesters, they could die by going outside. If you view Uhlfelder's actions through a scientific lens, they don't make sense. Only when you recognize them for the political ploy they are do they reveal what's really going on.

The internal contradictions of the Party of Science™ were exposed when President Trump refused to empower the central government to make all the decisions about the virus. Red and blue states would have to enact their own policies, giving Americans a true demonstration of what each party really believed and what that would look like in practice.

Here's what it looked like: in many blue states, arbitrary rules dictated by political considerations, while in many red states, local control was customized to the specific needs of communities.

So what did the guidance for outdoor gatherings look like in states with governors who subscribe to the strong central government theory of management?

Despite a growing body of evidence that breathing recirculated indoor air was perhaps more risky than outdoor transmission, blue state governors embraced draconian restrictions on outdoor gatherings. And they would enforce them—with the exception of certain protesters with whom their political views aligned.

Beaches were closed in Virginia. Golf courses shuttered in Massachusetts, Washington, and many other states. Surfing was allowed on the same beach where swimming was prohibited in Maryland. An outdoor skate park was filled with sand in California. Boating was prohibited in Michigan. In Washington State, drive-through automatic car washes were ruled to be unsafe, with Democratic governor Jay Inslee turning down a safety plan to allow them to reopen.

My family visited Sullivan's Island off the coast of South Carolina in mid-August, when many southern states were reopening following the July COVID spike. We brought our two small grandchildren and their parents with us. We were greeted by a confusing array of rules that precluded us from bringing chairs, coolers, or any item that could provide shade. Skin cancer—no problem. Dehydration—go for it. Heatstroke—will probably happen. Just government making all the decisions.

Meanwhile, early studies out of China published in early April suggested outdoor transmission of the virus was rare. In one study, China found just two cases among 318 outbreaks in which outdoor transmission could be documented.

Michigan governor Gretchen Whitmer discouraged outdoor gardening, going so far as to prohibit the sale of seeds in local grocery stores during the spring planting season. In early April, a father in Colorado was handcuffed and arrested in front of his six-year-old daughter after playing tee-ball in a public park on a Sunday afternoon. His crime? Violating social distancing restrictions. In Pennsylvania around the same time, a nineteen-year-old woman was ticketed for two hundred dollars after she was pulled over and admitted to "going for a drive." She was arrested for failing to abide by the order of the governor and secretary of health to control the spread of a communicable disease.

People who gathered to watch the sunset on closed California beaches and trails were ticketed. Encinitas mayor Catherine Blakespear claimed the enforcement was necessary to "save lives" and keep people safe. In Malibu, a solo paddleboarder was chased down by police in a boat and arrested for violating Governor Gavin Newsom's stay-at-home order.

Even more frustrating was the hypocrisy with which elected officials flouted their own orders. In California, Governor Newsom shut down wineries in nineteen counties, but excluded the county in which his own winery was located. In Michigan, Governor Whitmer ordered residents to avoid boating or using their second homes during the lockdown. But in the days after she loosened that restriction, her own husband tried to use his connection to her to jump to the front of the line to get his boat in the water before Memorial Day weekend.

None of this was based in science.

Nevertheless, governors and progressives had harsh words for people who gathered outdoors for Memorial Day weekend after being cooped up in their homes for months.

That weekend, a photo went viral showing a packed outdoor

gathering at Lake of the Ozarks in Missouri. Just four days before Black Lives Matter protests would break out across the nation, some of which would last well into the summer, former Missouri Democratic senator Claire McCaskill tweeted her disgust at those assembled at Lake of the Ozarks. "Embarrassing for my state," she wrote. "Hope none of them have parents fighting cancer, grandparents with diabetes, aunts and uncles with serious heart conditions. Because clearly they could care less."

Four days later, you'd have been hard-pressed to find a Democratic governor who didn't care less than those Ozarks partiers. The number of governors who participated in or sanctioned the Black Lives Matter protests after condemning and restricting such gatherings for months was breathtaking. In New Jersey, Governor Phil Murphy marched with protesters in violation of his own order. In New Mexico, Democratic governor Michelle Lujan Grisham justified the protests, saying, "This is a violation of the mass gatherings, no doubt, but we're just going to take a leap of faith in protecting protesters who have no other way, quite frankly. Right? There's no other way to be seen, to be heard, to be respected, and to be clear about your message."

Several weeks would pass before the *New York Times* got around to covering the discordant messaging between lockdown protests and Black Lives Matter protests. In a July 6 piece titled "Are Protests Dangerous? What Experts Say May Depend on Who's Protesting What," the paper acknowledged the hypocrisy of public health officials over the protests.

They cited journalist and essayist Thomas Chatterton Williams, who wrote, "The way the public health narrative around coronavirus has reversed itself overnight seems an awful lot like . . . politicizing science."

You think?

Undermining the Experts

The impact of all of this is, of course, to undermine the credibility of science and public health expertise. We don't know the long-term impacts of that strategy, but they are likely to dwarf any short-term benefits gained in the election.

Perhaps Fox News' Tucker Carlson summed it up best:

> This is insanity. It is definitely not science. This is not science. It has nothing to do with the public's health, much less the broader public interest. This is instead what happens when mediocre people suddenly find themselves with God-like power: deciding who can go outside, when people can get married, which medical procedures you're allowed to have. That's a feeling of omnipotence, and they like that feeling. It fills an empty place inside. They don't want to give it up. They want it to last forever, even as the country dies. But it can't last forever. Because it's not their country. It's ours.

Therein lies the danger of a strong central government. In theory, the laws they apply will be grounded in science and implemented with an eye to public health. But in practice, the politics of power are the fuel for these decisions. Americans have an innate and well-founded distrust in unchecked power for this very reason. Which is why, appeals to science notwithstanding, we must resist the efforts of politicians to use crises as a pretext to violate our constitutionally protected natural rights.

CHAPTER 4

A POLITICIZED TRAGEDY

Using fear of a tragedy to push a political agenda is hardly a new innovation. Obama chief of staff Rahm Emanuel's advice to Democrats was to "never let a serious crisis go to waste." And they haven't.

Never let it be said that politicians let the coronavirus crisis or the racial tensions of 2020 go to waste. Countless pet policies suddenly became the urgent solution to the pain Americans were feeling. Emanuel at the time described crises as "an opportunity to do things that you could not do before."

In its full context, the Emanuel quotation was actually aspirational and laudable. He described an opportunity for both sides to come together to solve problems instead of kicking the can down the road. But his words aren't remembered that way. Because it didn't happen that way. The Obama administration quickly took advantage of a deep national recession to justify policies that were not just unhelpful, but economically counterproductive. His economic stimulus package included dubious solutions such as state government bailouts, credits for home efficiency projects, and generous loan guarantees for renewable energy companies, many of which would fail. One such company, Solyndra, got half a billion taxpayer dollars, then filed for bankruptcy two years later. But only after the Obama Department of Energy agreed to restructure the loan under terms favorable to politically connected stakeholders. The term ensured Obama fund-raising bundler and Tulsa billionaire George Kaiser was guaranteed millions in future tax breaks in the event of a bankruptcy. Meanwhile, national unemployment rates continued to climb, going from 8.3 percent to 10 percent within six months of the bill's passage. It would take a global pandemic to reach those heights again.

The Obama administration went on to dramatically raise out-of-pocket health care costs for working Americans, increase taxes for everyone, significantly increase fiscal burdens to local governments they had just bailed out, penalize investment, and drastically expand the regulatory state. Though these policies created a drag on the economy, the administration used the recession to justify the urgent need for them, not even bothering with a pretense of seeking support or input from those across the aisle.

For Beltway politicians, the recession's silver lining was the opportunity to do something they couldn't do before—to capitalize on people's fears; to pass something that couldn't pass without the urgency of a major threat—and a threatening enemy.

Which brings us to 2020. It was a year that ushered in a reality most of us never imagined we would live to see: a disease we were told would spread unchecked to millions, the forced closure of the vaunted American economy, a virtual standstill of the global travel industry, violence in our streets on a scale many cities had never seen before, and the most controversial general election of most of our lifetimes. All aided and encouraged by a lockdown-loving political, cultural, academic, and media elite. We saw jobs lost, schools closed, primary elections canceled, professional sports halted, funerals forbidden, and churchgoers harassed. We saw black store owners looted, black police as-saulted, and statues to black advocates torn down in the name of racial justice.

The combination of a virus that was projected to kill millions of Americans and a Republican president running for reelection on the basis of a strong economy created the perfect environment for the left to leverage a catastrophe.

A familiar script would play out over and over again as disas-ter liberalism made the most of what 2020 had to offer. Divisions that had not previously been partisan would become politicized. We would be told to defer to experts, who would tell us which solutions would work. And those experts would dutifully inform us that the only way out of our current predicament was to en-act the same progressive policy prescriptions Pelosi had tried and failed to pass for years. Partisan enemies would be created to inspire fear and a sense of urgency. MAGA cap–wearing kids, billionaires getting rich off the lockdown, churchgoing Chris-tians, legal gun owners, privileged white people raised in nuclear families, and inner-city cops would all be cast as the villains in a liberal tragedy that only bigger government could repair.

As the lockdowns began to impact pocketbooks, the question of how and when to end the lockdowns became openly parti-san. Normally, Miles's law applies—the notion that "where you stand depends on where you sit." People aligned themselves for or against economic closures based on how those closures would affect them personally, not based on partisan identity or their opinions of President Trump.

We could argue whether the question became politicized when President Trump aligned himself with a strong economy or when Democrats reflexively aligned in favor of aggressive lock-downs. But once the question became politicized, the partisan characterization stuck. The way in which people responded to the virus became a virtue signal (or a vice signal, if you will) of their political views.

According to the narrative espoused by Democrats and their acolytes, Trump supporters who wanted to reopen the economy put dollars over lives and didn't care if people died. Everyone who cared about public health opposed Trump and supported the lockdowns. Of course, that wasn't really true. Miles's law still applied. Trump supporters weren't the only ones suffering from the economic impact of the response to the virus. But it didn't matter. That was the narrative. An aggressive response to the virus allegedly aligned with an aggressive campaign to oust the president, and the president's enemies saw a big opportunity to leverage the crisis to promote their agenda.

In government, in academia, in media, and in other bastions of progressivism, the worst-case scenarios became the reality. Only the most extreme response would do. Beginning in blue cities and blue states, stay-at-home orders restricted businesses from operating. Businesses weren't given the option, in many cases, of adapting to CDC social distancing guidelines. They were simply told to close and were penalized if they refused.

It was a dangerous environment that created all the wrong incentives. Our response to the virus should have been focused on good science and a clear-eyed analysis of the trade-offs, not on who might win an election six months out. Nonetheless, good news was often suppressed, bad news was amplified, and the term "fear porn" was used by the right to describe the glee with which the left seemed to greet worst-case scenarios about the virus.

The Cost of Politicizing Tragedy

When George W. Bush presided over the worst terrorist attack in American history, the nation and the world came together to mourn, to defend America, and to fight back. For me, like most

Americans, those weeks following the destruction of the World Trade Center were both a painful and a sacred time of unity and resolve.

I'll never forget sitting with our young kids, who didn't understand what was going on, and explaining the evil that had changed the world overnight. People all over the globe came together, helping in their own way. For their part, my little kids made macaroni necklaces and scribbled thank-you cards in crayon to send to first responders. Julie and I each wrote our own letters to first responders, who were left mourning their dead and reeling from the enormity of what was still ahead. We didn't know exactly where to send our care package, but we found an address for the New York City Fire Department and popped our expressions of gratitude in the mail. I hope they got them. I hope they felt how much we appreciated and cared about them, even two thousand miles away.

We weren't alone. Such things were happening all around the country. It was a testament to the American spirit. When the worst happens, the best show up.

But not this time.

There were still those making masks to donate, sharing their food and toilet paper during shortages, and reaching out to lonely neighbors. That is the American way. But 2020 wasn't like 2001.

Americans had responded to 9/11 by hanging flags from our homes, honoring our first responders, and celebrating our nation's resilience. Midway through 2020, many would be doing the opposite: burning flags, assaulting first responders, and denouncing the rights and freedoms we once celebrated. Unlike the devastation of September 11, 2001, which was graphic and immediate, the impacts of the crises of 2020 were disparate, slow moving, and easily politicized. While 9/11 took place after a major presidential election, this disaster played out during a divisive one. Instead of uniting against terrorists, we were divided over whether it was "racist" to even acknowledge the source of the virus. Instead of celebrating potential new treatments, Americans picked sides, rooting for or against the success of a treatment based on which presidential campaign would benefit.

Each side seemed to have its own science. With the virus new and untested, the lack of scientific consensus created greater opportunities to politicize the response to the virus. It seemed whatever position President Trump took, the opposing party (and even some within his own party) would take the opposite. In some cases, the differences represented sincere political divisions. In others, they seemed arbitrary. Since President Trump had been running on the strong economy, Democrats opted to run with a pro-lockdown message. When President Trump speculated about the potential for a new treatment using the inexpensive and widely available drug hydroxychloroquine, Democrats became invested in the belief that the treatment would fail. When Trump supporters wanted to exercise their constitutional right to assemble and protest the lockdowns, the left objected. When the left wanted to exercise those same rights to protest police brutality, racism, capitalism, or American history, or to celebrate gay pride, suddenly large gatherings were okay again.

The left fought Trump every step of the way, even when his proposals represented the best policy, as when he closed the U.S. to travelers from China. Facts didn't matter. Only narratives— the stories politicians could get people to believe. It didn't matter what position Trump took. They would object.

For their part, Trump and his supporters did the same. When the left pushed for mask mandates, instead of simply objecting to the notion of a mandate, a few on the right rebelled against the notion of wearing masks at all. If one side reversed their position, the other side reversed theirs. Politicizing the virus incentivized people to ignore or distort the science in the pursuit of political ends.

The Absolute Power of Donald J. Trump

Perhaps the most obvious example of how politicized the crisis had become happened in mid-April, when President Trump stunned viewers of his then-daily press briefings with a claim that nearly everyone disputed.

"When somebody is president of the United States the authority is total, and that's the way it's got to be," he said.

"The authority is total?" asked an incredulous reporter.

"It's total. And the governors know that," he responded.

In fact, most conservatives had been arguing presidential authority was not total. It had been the left urging the president to take a more authoritarian approach. As proponents of federalism, conservatives had been supportive of a strategy that empowered governors to make decisions for their own states. The Tenth Amendment to the Constitution is clear that powers not explicitly delegated to the federal government are reserved to the states. We didn't want a national mask mandate—not because masks were bad, but because the Constitution doesn't authorize the federal government to dictate such policies. It should be left to the states. Which is what President Trump did. But in this moment, it wasn't what he said.

The president's statement set off a scramble as each side now wrestled with how to defend a position they had vocally opposed for weeks. Up until that press conference, Trump had taken heavy criticism for failing to issue a national stay-at-home order. His leadership had been questioned because he didn't implement the kind of one-size-fits-all, cookie-cutter approach that the left favors.

It's rather entertaining now to go back and read the headlines and social media posts from the week prior to Trump's April 13 claim of absolute authority.

The *Washington Post*, three days earlier, ran a story head-lined, "A Plan to Defeat Coronavirus Finally Emerges, but It's Not from the White House." The article seemed to promote the notion that Trump had broad authority, but he just wasn't using it. The story contained an explosive claim that would set leftist tongues wagging:

> Administration officials, speaking on the condition of anonymity to describe internal deliberations, say the White House has made a deliberate political calculation that it will better serve Trump's interest to put the onus on governors—rather than the federal government—to figure out how to move ahead.

Immediately, that paragraph of the story (not a quotation) went viral. CNN's Brian Stelter tweeted it out, writing, "Let that quote sink in . . ." In response, numerous people replied, "Federalism. How does it work?" One Twitter user facetiously reframed the argument, writing, "Ugh. Why can't Trump be more authoritarian?"

The Federalist's Mollie Hemingway was more specific, replying:

> Yes, the U.S. Constitution is a hundreds-year-long plot to help Trump win re-election. Excellent take. Also, it's not a "quote" but an unsupported assertion based on reporters' dubious and unverifiable interpretation of what they claim anon sources told them.

She was right. The paragraph is not a direct quotation from a Trump staffer. The reader has no way of knowing whether the use of the word "calculation"—which implies more cynical motives—came from the source or from the reporter.

In fact, the president had been anything but authoritarian in his approach, consistently empowering governors to customize their approach to the needs of their residents as the Constitution so brilliantly establishes. But even as the left complained of Trump's failure to impose an authoritarian approach, they bafflingly continued to criticize him for being an authoritarian.

Typical of the tweets we saw during the week leading up to President Trump's assertion of total authority was an April 10 post from Jennifer Mercieca, a rhetoric professor and author of the book *Demagogue for President*. Mercieca tweeted:

> Trump has done nothing to stop the virus, has not organized a national response to stop the virus, and has no plan to stop the virus or organize a national response to stop the virus. And yet he wants your attention for press conferences about the virus.

The view that Trump had failed because he hadn't single-handedly imposed a monolithic solution on a nation of nearly 330 million people was widespread. Economist David Rothschild tweeted a similar sentiment on April 11, writing:

> After #70days of inaction led to 2,000+ death/day, President Trump still has no plan for ending outbreak in US AND no plan for how to safely reopen economy. We need testing, tracing, masks, worker relief, not empty platitudes from an incompetent & corrupt wannabe authoritarian.

That one was a head scratcher for me. It wasn't President Trump's job to make all of the decisions. That's what an authoritarian dictator would do. But because he didn't do that, he is a corrupt wannabe authoritarian? I can't understand why leftists who believed Trump to be incompetent would have even wanted him making all of the decisions. But because he didn't, he was criticized for having no plan.

Meanwhile, Trump continued to be criticized for taking on

too much power. Author Richard North Patterson went even further, writing of Trump in the *Bulwark*, "COVID-19 has metastasized his authoritarian pathologies."

Two days later, Trump would claim total authority and people on the left would lose their minds. The irony of calling the man an authoritarian for failing to act like one seemed to be lost on most leftists at the time. But if that seemed unhinged, the response to Trump's new assertion of total authority—an assertion they had been virtually begging him to make—was even more mystifying. Granted, the context of his remarks was about his authority to reopen economies, not, as leftists had wished, for him to unilaterally keep them closed. Still, it was the approach many had been demanding in which the federal government runs roughshod over the states and individual rights.

It was anti-American. It was likely unconstitutional. And now Trump was seemingly embracing it. Would the left welcome the president's new recognition of their preferred role for him? Or would they reverse course, making Trump's previous arguments for him? It was a no-win situation.

Whatever Trump's reasons for making the incredible claim of absolute authority, this incident ultimately put his opponents right where he wanted them. Instead of having to make the arguments for federalism himself, leftists and their media enablers would make the arguments for him. And they did.

CNN tweeted, "Facts First: The President does not have 'total' authority over coronavirus restrictions. There is no legislation that explicitly gives the President the power to override states' public health measures." Isn't that exactly what the right had been arguing up to that point? That President Trump didn't have the authority to impose a nationwide stay-at-home order or to require people to wear masks?

In truth, the limits of the president's authority in a crisis are not well defined. Just how much authority does a president have under such extraordinary circumstances? These were unprecedented times. David Marcus speculated in *The Federalist* about what Trump could possibly gain from a blanket assertion of authority that he had to know was, at best, undefined. In short, leverage. Marcus concluded:

> Does Trump have the authority to end the lockdowns in the states? I'm no expert, but probably not. Most of the experts say probably not. Cuomo says in his opinion the president has no such authority. In his opinion, though, he used those words for a reason. Nobody really knows. And until we have to find out, and hopefully we never do, President Trump should concede nothing on this issue. Neither he nor the country will gain anything if the executive branch of the federal government raises the white flag in surrender.

Whatever President Trump's reasons for taking that position, the event exposed one thing: in the response to COVID-19, the driving force is not principle, but power.

A Tale of Two Approaches

The approach taken by President Trump in response to the virus was the opposite of disaster liberalism. Instead of capitalizing on the opportunity for a power grab or leveraging the disaster to accelerate the enactment of unrelated policy priorities, Trump employed a federalist approach that empowered governors to decide.

There were trade-offs to this approach. If one assumes the experts had all the answers from the beginning, then this approach precluded those "right" answers from being implemented uniformly. But given how little we knew about the virus, the federalist approach had the advantage of enabling the laboratory of ideas to experiment with a range of approaches that could provide valuable information for later pandemic responses.

Not surprisingly, blue states tended to favor more restrictive lockdowns and constitutionally questionable limits on individual rights. Red state governors were more likely to minimize business closures and accelerate the lifting of restrictions.

In the days before Trump claimed absolute authority, Michigan governor Gretchen Whitmer extended Michigan's stay-at-home order through the end of April as case counts spiked in her state. As Democrats criticized the president for failing to impose a one-size-fits-all solution on the whole country, I wondered—would Michigan Democrats have preferred an approach that allowed the president to override Whitmer's order?

Kentucky Democratic governor Andy Beshear had state police out recording the license plate numbers of vehicles seen at mass gatherings over the weekend so that he could send local health officials to contact them and require them to self-quarantine for fourteen days. In Texas, Republican governor Greg Abbott was preparing an executive order to reopen his state's economy.

Imagine a world in which a Democrat is president during such a time. We don't have to imagine because we had that in 2009. But no one demanded of Barack Obama what they have demanded of Donald Trump. So suspend disbelief for a moment and imagine that the president really did take the authoritarian approach of dictating to every state, district, and territory what their lockdown and reopening policies should be.

Long term, does anyone really want to live in a country like that? Do the Democrats even want that? Surely these Democratic governors would not want President Trump dictating to their states—either to lock down or to reopen? I can imagine such an edict having been grounds for yet another round of impeachment proceedings.

But if we had had a Democrat in the Oval Office in 2020, and if (big if) she were willing to impose a nationwide lockdown on states, would even the bluest of states be happy with that? I don't think so.

In truth, we all know federalism is the best approach.

The push for President Trump to take an authoritarian approach wasn't about public health. Does anyone believe Democrats would have been supportive of restrictive public health mandates from the Trump administration? It wasn't about good policy. It was about leveraging a crisis for political advantage. In this case, it was an opportunity to discredit Donald Trump in time for the presidential election. Americans who lost livelihoods, whose health was impacted, whose lives were at stake— they were just collateral damage.

By deferring to states, President Trump unleashed the laboratory of ideas. Instead of a one-size-fits-all approach, he chose to embrace the federalist system that is the foundation of America. As this book goes to print, we don't have all the details about how that experiment ultimately played out. Did red states or blue states fare better? Did governors who locked down get better results than governors who didn't? But we do know that by the time the election rolled around, the virus was spreading uncontained around the world. The timing of the spikes varied, but the trajectory of the outbreak did not. Nations that appeared to have contained the virus were again seeing an alarming rise in case counts. Blue states and red states were all seeing similar spikes, regardless of how restrictive their lockdowns had been.

I expect we'll see a lot of analysis on those questions. Did the lockdowns work? And were they worth it? In the next pandemic—and there is always a next pandemic—we need to be ready with the answers to those questions. Otherwise our response will be driven by whoever can best leverage the disaster for political gain.

If lockdowns worked, we would see case counts drop within weeks of restrictions being imposed and we would expect to see them climb shortly after states reopened for business. Instead, we saw a similar curve in every state—steep climbs as the virus spread, followed by a leveling out, and eventually a slow drop. The timing of those curves varied but was never consistently connected to the onset of lockdowns or the lifting of restrictions.

But even if, months from now, we discover that lockdowns worked, that restrictions on speech, religion, assembly, gun rights, privacy, due process, and federalism were the price of defeating the virus, what happens next? Once we surrender the rights our forefathers so zealously protected, what does America look like then? Some might argue that the emergency suspension of constitutional rights is no long-term threat to American freedom and liberty. But the empirical trajectory of modern liberalism is a slippery slope.

CHAPTER 5

THE INEVITABLE SLIPPERY SLOPE OF LIBERALISM

Three years before mobs of Black Lives Matter protesters began toppling monuments and tagging public buildings with graffiti following the death of George Floyd, President Trump was roundly ridiculed for predicting what has now become fact—that the targeting of Confederate statues would lead to the targeting of Founding Fathers. Incredulous news outlets in 2017 responded indignantly to Trump's prediction by citing historians, academics, and pundits who assured Americans that removing statues of Confederate figures was a far cry from going after the Fathers of our country.

The August 2017 white nationalist Unite the Right rally in Charlottesville, Virginia, had become violent, with one woman being killed and others injured. The debate over removing Confederate monuments had been one of the key disputes in a conflict that would serve as a prelude to the brutality of 2020.

President Trump responded at the time, horrifying political adversaries with his statement. "This week it's Robert E. Lee," he said. "I notice that Stonewall Jackson's coming down. I wonder, is it George Washington next week and is it Thomas Jefferson the week after?" That comment created an uproar as offended leftists lined up to denounce such a bad take. The preposterous notion that the Founding Fathers might come under attack was ridiculed by scholars and pundits alike.

Those takes became a lot more interesting in 2020 than they had been in 2017. One of my favorite publications, *The Federalist*, published a devastating retrospective of the 2017 media fallout. The author of the piece, my Fox News colleague Mollie Hemingway, cited many of the very properly aggrieved and not-at-all-biased stories responding to Trump's statement.

She cited a *New York Times* piece headlined, "Historians Question Trump's Comments on Confederate Monuments." One historian is cited in the story calling Trump's argument a "red herring" while another said, "The answer to Mr. Trump's hypothetical question about whether getting rid of Lee and Jackson also meant junking Washington and Jefferson was a simple 'no.'"

George Washington University history professor Denver Brunsman, whose university has now removed a bust of its namesake after it was toppled by rioters, was among those scoffing at the president in 2017. He told the *Washington Post* at the time that removing Confederate statues was not the same as going after Washington because Washington's vision of America was "quite different from the vision of the Confederacy, which was founded on the premise of slavery forevermore." The same story cited Jim Grossman, executive director of the American Historical Association, calling Trump's suggestion "absurd" and "unacceptable from the President of the United States."

It seems the *Post* couldn't find a single historian who could conceive of monuments to Founding Fathers ever being put at risk. "It's the difference between a monument to the founder of our nation, and a monument to a key figure in an effort to break apart the nation," said University of Virginia faculty member and Pulitzer Prize–winning journalist Douglas Blackmon. "The most kind explanation of that can only be ignorance, and I don't say that to insult the president."

Juxtaposed against a backdrop of monuments to Founding Fathers and civil rights defenders alike coming under attack in early summer 2020, it's clear President Trump could see the path ahead far better than those who study the path behind.

There's a name for such jumps. It's called a slippery slope—a small step in one direction that results in a steep fall toward an unintended or unacceptable result. President Trump understood the danger of the slippery slope. Which may partially explain why he was reluctant to embrace the slippery slope of suspending constitutional rights during a pandemic.

Nevertheless, the slippery-slope argument wasn't lost on Trump's critics. Hemingway's story went on to cite Jamelle Bouie of *Slate*, who called Trump's comments "dumb." "It doesn't really even make any sense," he said. "And the notion that there's some slippery slope is dumb." Bouie wasn't the only one to dismiss the argument out of hand. Hemingway dug up a report from NBC News quoting Boston historian Kevin Levin. The article questioned, "Is the president right about the impending threat to the founders? Historians who spoke to NBC News said such fears are slightly misplaced and that Trump is championing a murky interpretation of history." The article quoted Levin saying, "The president can raise the slippery slope, but it's a false slippery slope."

It wasn't.

In 2020, no one was laughing as Trump's slippery-slope predictions materialized across the nation. A key problem with liberalism as a motivating philosophy is that it does not have a limiting principle. It deconstructs traditions and seizes power gleefully—and once the barriers are down and the power is seized, good luck getting back to the way things were. We can see that in the way liberals happily toppled statues without heed to history or tradition.

Erasing History

George Washington, who could have been king and instead chose to submit himself to elections, was basically being canceled because he owned slaves. A Portland, Oregon, mob in June 2020 wrapped a flag over the face of a Washington statue in their city, using it as tinder to light the likeness aflame. By morning, the statue was toppled, its base covered in graffiti denigrating people on the basis of their skin color. Messages like "White fragility," "Defund white men," and "Damn white men" apparently don't meet the progressive definition of racism. It wasn't a one-off. Other Washington statues were defaced in Baltimore, Chicago, and on the campus of George Washington University. Renewed calls to destroy Mount Rushmore accompanied President Trump's iconic visit to the landmark over Independence Day weekend.

President Trump in 2017 originally mentioned not just Washington, but the third president of the United States, Thomas Jefferson. Jefferson's statue at the university he founded, Charlottesville's University of Virginia, had repeatedly been the target of vandals over the years. But leftist attacks on Jefferson intensified during the endless weeks and months of Black Lives Matter protests. Members of the New York City Council called to remove City Hall's statue of Thomas Jefferson, despite the fact that his undisputed role in the writing of the Declaration of Independence built support for what would become the most free and prosperous nation in world history. In June 2020, a mob tore down a Thomas Jefferson statue at Jefferson High School in Portland. Another statue at Virginia's College of William & Mary, Jefferson's alma mater, was defaced.

The slope got steeper as statues of India's Mahatma Gandhi, Union general Ulysses S. Grant, and national anthem author Francis Scott Key were senselessly defaced or toppled.

By the Fourth of July weekend, no historical figure, regardless of the watershed events they facilitated, seemed immune from the mobs. Vandals chose Independence Day weekend to rip from its base the statue of revered abolitionist and former slave Frederick Douglass in Rochester, New York—a site of the Underground Railroad. This, on the 168th anniversary of his famous July 5, 1852, speech, "What to the slave is the Fourth of July."

The end of the slippery slope is a world where we cannot celebrate the accomplishments, no matter how great, of human beings who do not exemplify modern political views.

In Philadelphia, a statue of famous abolitionist Matthias Baldwin was vandalized. The man who dedicated his life to educating young black children was labeled a "colonizer" in graffiti. *National Review* quoted Joe Walsh, a member of the Friends of Matthias Baldwin Park, saying this of the man who fought for the right of African Americans to vote in Pennsylvania: "He was BLM before there was a slogan." The headline in *The Federalist* could have been from the satirical *Babylon Bee*: "'Social Justice Warriors, Deface Statues of Actual Social Justice Warriors." No historical figure was safe. They went after Abraham Lincoln, who literally freed the slaves. In Boston, protesters even defaced a monument to the all-black volunteer 54th Massachusetts Regiment of the Union Army.

I don't object to reconsidering the identity of statues we erect. There are legitimate arguments to be made that some Confederate memorials were erected by Klan forces to intimidate the local black population in an earlier era. Communities have every right to soberly evaluate who is represented in public art for any reason.

I wholeheartedly supported an effort in Utah to swap out a statue of television inventor Philo Farnsworth in the U.S. Capitol with that of Martha Hughes Cannon, the first female state senator in the United States. There was nothing wrong with Farnsworth, but a group called Better Days 2020 initiated a public process to make a change because many Utahns felt it was appropriate to recognize a pioneering lawmaker during the anniversary of women's suffrage. Each state gets just two statues in the Capitol and only nine of those one hundred statues are women. Women in Utah, to their credit, pushed hard to make the swap that will bring Farnsworth home to Utah, despite his important accomplishments, and send Cannon to be Utah's second statue and also the tenth statue representing a woman in the U.S. Capitol. The process was public, deliberate, and transparent.

As the fourth wife of a polygamist, Cannon held values that many consider anathema to current social practices. But the people of Utah believe the inspiring story of a pioneering medical doctor who defeated her own husband in 1896 to become America's first female state senator is worth representing in public art.

Such processes are valuable. However, these decisions should not be left to mobs and vandals. In particular, the choice to erase imperfect people in our history is a slippery slope that Venezuelan immigrant Elizabeth Rogliani has seen before. Following the destruction of historical statues in June, Rogliani warned Americans against duplicating the path her country began a decade ago. In an interview with Fox News' Laura Ingraham, Rogliani sounded an alarm to her friends who think the statue debate is harmless:

> Why do I even worry about some silly little statues coming down or some silly little street names changing? Why do I care? It is because the last time I didn't care about this, I was a teenager.
>
> I have already lived through this thing when I was living in Venezuela. Statues came down, [Hugo] Chavez didn't want the history displayed. Then he changed the street names, then came the curriculum, then some movies couldn't be shown on certain TV channels.

You guys think it can't happen to you. I've heard this so many times. But always be on guard, never believe that something can't happen to you. You need to guard your country and your society or it will be destroyed. . . . And there's clearly a lot of people wanting to destroy the U.S.

Sure enough, the war on history didn't end with removing Confederate statues, Founding Father statues, or any other statues. The left continued to move the goalposts with demands to change the names of American cities, streets, schools, and military bases. In June 2020, thousands signed a petition to rename Columbus, Ohio, after the famous catchphrase of native Guy Fieri. The city would become Flavortown, Ohio, if signers got their way. Despite the role of Christopher Columbus in one of the greatest watershed events of human history, he cannot be forgiven for being a product of his time.

Even books that accurately reflect ugly racism in our history began to be banned. Minnesota has banned classic literature, including *To Kill a Mockingbird* and *Huckleberry Finn*, from use in schools because they accurately depict ugly historic realities of race. President Trump's prediction that Washington and Jefferson would be next was not only correct, but it actually fell short. Since then, we've seen calls to blow up Mount Rushmore, destroy monuments on the National Mall, cancel our national Fourth of July celebration, and replace our national anthem. The progressive movement has declared war on patriotism in America, insisting that we disregard the achievements of the world's most successful government experiment.

This is what is meant by a slippery slope. The first step is often reasonable. Let's reconsider whether we need so many monuments to Confederate leaders. Of course we should. But what lies at the end of that road? As more and more history is erased, more and more voices are silenced, and more and more narratives rewritten, the nation has been pulled further and further from reality, to a place where the lessons of history cannot be learned and the successes of the past cannot be replicated.

The same is true of the national response to the global pandemic. What started out as a reasonable response morphed into a catastrophic overreaction. Liberalism has no limiting principle. It is for this reason that conservatives stand opposed to endless "progress."

How Fifteen Days to Stop the Spread Became Endless Lockdown

If we hadn't learned it yet, the pandemic response provided another lesson in the old axiom—give them an inch and they'll take a mile. Per the usual pattern, this slippery slope began with an entirely rational request. In the face of a worldwide contagion, we all needed to stay at home. Of course we did. That is a reasonable response to a communicable disease. President Trump had already shut down travel from affected countries in Asia and Europe. The next logical step was to contain the spread.

But the devil was in the details, and the same partisan divisions that animated debates between the Federalist and Anti-Federalist Founding Fathers continue to bedevil American leaders today. When it comes to a solution, does one size fit all? Or should communities be free to customize solutions to their own unique circumstances? Should the problem be solved by the force of a strong central government, by delegation of power to the states, or by voluntary compliance? If a one-size-fits-all solution works better than a patchwork of different standards, is it worth the trade-off in liberty and individual rights and the precedent that it would set? We didn't have the luxury of debating those questions with a deadly virus bearing down.

Some businesses closed voluntarily. Others, like airlines,

simply had few customers to serve as so many people stayed home. But mandatory closures were coming. Had we known what that would look like in practice, perhaps we would have been less sanguine about it.

In retrospect, it is stunning how quickly and easily we surrendered our constitutional rights. But it's easy to see how it happened. The reason was sound: the need was temporary and the alternative was potentially bleak. So we allowed government to infringe on our property, our lawful contracts, and our due process rights. Just this once.

It was just supposed to be fifteen days to stop the spread, according to President Trump and White House health advisor Dr. Anthony Fauci. That would be painful, but worthwhile if it prevented people from dying.

We gave government an inch. Government would quickly take a mile.

The Power Grab

When I wrote my last book, titled *Power Grab*, I understood that individual liberties were an impediment to the progressive agenda. It was something I saw up close as a member of Congress. Freedom and liberty are not very compatible with the level of force required to impose one-size-fits-all approaches from a strong central government. Force is required to implement redistributive policies and sky-high taxes required to maintain an all-powerful state. I predicted that once given access to the levers of power, Democrats would leverage that power to secure power more permanently, to stack the deck in their favor, and to remove impediments to the powerful central government they revered. But despite that perspective, even I have been shocked at the brazenness with which elected officials leveraged the crises of 2020 to rule their constituents rather than govern them.

There were a number of predictable questions raised in my mind once we agreed to surrender certain rights during a pandemic. When we agreed that government had the power to shut down the economy, force businesses to close, and penalize noncompliance, there would be long-term implications. First, what if fifteen days was not enough to stop the spread? What was the limit to how long government could keep the country locked down?

Second, once the guardrails protecting our rights were removed, what would prevent abuses of power from careening out of control? Was there any limiting principle on a governor or mayor now that constitutional rights were expected to be waived?

Finally, what recourse did Americans have when their elected leaders went too far? What would the judiciary enforce in a time of national emergency?

All of these questions will be the subject of lawsuits in the aftermath of a catastrophic economic lockdown. Hundreds of legal challenges are working their way through courts in nearly every state. Ballotpedia compiles an ongoing list of lawsuits challenging state actions and policies related to the pandemic. By October 2020, that list was approaching a thousand lawsuits across the country.

Some of the earliest challenges have already rebuked overreaching governors. The Wisconsin Supreme Court struck down Democratic governor Tony Evers's "Safer at Home" orders in May. In Michigan, the state supreme court slapped down executive orders issued by first-term governor Gretchen Whitmer, ruling she did not have authority to renew executive orders past April 30, 2020, under the state's Emergency Management Act. In Pennsylvania, a federal court ruled that Democratic governor Tom Wolf's order violated constitutional rights of assembly and speech as well as Fourteenth Amendment rights of due process and equal protection.

On the other hand, the Oregon Supreme Court struck down a lower court ruling against Governor Kate Brown's lockdown orders, enabling her restrictions to remain in place. We can expect to see states take a closer look at their emergency powers provisions in the aftermath of 2020.

But we didn't need a prophet to predict that what started as an effort to stop the spread of disease could easily morph into a power grab.

For his part, President Trump passed up perhaps the easiest power grab since George Washington's refusal to be king. For all of the fretting about his authoritarian talk and tendencies, he didn't act like someone who wanted to seize more power or trample individual rights. Some elected officials certainly did, but Trump was not among them.

Perhaps we don't fully appreciate just how much power a true authoritarian president could have wielded during the crisis. President Trump could have taken upon himself power to pick winners and losers in American business, as Democratic governors soon did. He could have tried to reshape civil society to his own tastes, dictating the role of faith, the rule of law, and the role of nonprofits. He could have played the tyrant, using this newfound power to reward loyal constituencies, retaliate against political adversaries, and tilt the electoral playing field in his favor, as Speaker Pelosi would later attempt to do (a story we'll get to later). He could have enforced his own values across the entire nation. He didn't.

I shudder to think of how a Barack Obama or a Hillary Clinton would have reacted to this unprecedented slippery-slope opportunity. These same people who claimed the expertise to cut our health care costs and let us choose our own doctors would no doubt have used the pretext of a global pandemic to hand our private health care system over to government bureaucrats.

And speaking of bureaucrats, in a Democratic administration, the likes of James Comey, Andrew McCabe, Peter Strzok, and Lisa Page would all still be running the FBI. That agency under President Obama was already secretly tracking cell phone data of American citizens and maintaining a facial recognition database of law-abiding Americans. Imagine what they would do with the opportunity to install contact tracing and geolocation tracking on our phones.

Remember how President Obama leveraged the power of the Department of Justice (DOJ), the intelligence agencies, and even the IRS to secure electoral advantages for his party? I certainly do. I wrote two books about it. As chairman of the House Oversight Committee at the time, I had an intimate knowledge of what they did.

The Obama/Biden administration used the DOJ to stymie legitimate investigations into the Democratic Party's presidential nominee, Hillary Clinton, even going so far as to grant immunity to key witnesses. They used intelligence agencies to inappropriately secure FISA warrants to spy on the campaign of the opposing party's presidential nominee and to illegally spy on journalists like James Rosen and writers for the Associated Press. And they used the IRS to collect sensitive donor information and to prevent conservative political groups from participating in the 2012 presidential election. In that case, they even went so far as to physically destroy evidence under subpoena. And this is what Biden and Obama called a scandal-free administration!

Given the history of Democratic administrations, and of the party's nominee Hillary Clinton, we can only imagine what she would have done with an opportunity like a global pandemic. She would have given the Chinese government a free pass and let immigration run rampant. Does anyone believe she would have shut down our borders under any circumstances?

To the surprise of many, President Trump chose to honor the Constitution, pursuing a federalist approach that gave state and local leaders wide latitude to determine the best interests of their individual communities. In doing so, he incurred the criticism of big-government enthusiasts who accused him of not having a plan and failing to lead. They were mystified by his unwillingness to seize the vast powers up for grabs in a time of crisis.

Instead, Trump put the proverbial laboratory of ideas to work, allowing each state to customize solutions to its own population, according to its own economic needs, and in response to its own case counts. Trump rallied private sector partnerships faster than I've ever seen—an approach that would have conceivably been shunned by corporation-hating Democrats. American manufacturers lined up to produce personal protective equipment and ventilators, drug companies entered into public-private partnerships to produce COVID-19 tests and to develop vaccines, and American companies worked with the U.S. Department of Agriculture (USDA) to provide nutritious meals for children.

In March, the administration worked with the National Association of Manufacturers to engage some forty companies in the voluntary production of protective equipment, ventilators, and other supplies. They engaged the Department of Health and Human Services to fast-track approval for U.S. manufacturers like Honeywell to convert assembly lines to manufacture N-95 masks or other needed equipment. Working with the National Council of Textile Organizations, they put together a consortium of factories to produce millions of masks, gloves, and protective clothing. They reached out to FedEx CEO Fred Smith for help moving cargo to distribute test swabs and sample collection kits flown in from abroad on specially chartered military transports.

They went on to engage the USDA in the Meals to You program to partner with private sector food and beverage companies to provide one million meals per week to rural children during the pandemic. That effort involved the Baylor Collaborative on Hunger and Poverty, PepsiCo, McLane Global, and others. By mid-July nearly thirty million meals had been delivered.

The administration announced a partnership with the Ad Council, major media networks, and digital platforms to "effectively communicate accurate and timely information to the American people." NBCUniversal, ViacomCBS, iHeartMedia, and ABC/Walt Disney Television were all involved.

In May, the administration launched Project Airbridge to expedite the shipment of personal protective equipment supplies for frontline workers from overseas. The list of companies voluntarily collaborating with the administration in the war on coronavirus was long: Ford, 3M, GE Healthcare, Toyota, Chrysler, MyPillow, Ralph Lauren, Brooks Brothers, Under Armour, Bauer, HP, Apple, and Tesla all joined the effort.

In May, the administration announced Operation Warp Speed to partner the government, the scientific community, and the private sector in the expedited development of a coronavirus vaccine.

For Americans unhappy with the lockdown conditions to which they were subjected, this local control was good news. It meant the people making the decisions actually answered to them. When the decisions are made by Congress, any given American is a constituent to just three of the 535 people making the decision—their two senators and their single House member. If people think getting an appointment with their own House member is difficult, wait until they try to get an appointment with someone who doesn't represent them. It doesn't happen.

Likewise, when decisions are made by the president, Americans have to compete with 330 million other people for the president's attention. The chances of getting a meeting, or a phone call, or a chance to lobby a member of the president's staff are logistically limited. But when decisions are made at the state and local levels, we all have more access to the decision makers. In some cases, they are our neighbors. In most cases, they depend on our vote to get reelected. Our ability to communicate with those leaders is greater and our opportunity to protest against them more effective. By properly delegating authority to state leaders, President Trump prevented our individual rights from being trampled—at least by him.

Once state leaders began wielding authority, Americans were treated to a real-time demonstration of the differences that animate the partisan divide in this country. On one side, leftist governors and mayors who sincerely believed government was the solution. On the other, right-leaning leaders who sincerely believed in empowering individuals and communities to find the solutions that worked for them.

In theory, a uniform, top-down solution could work. In many countries—smaller countries—it worked well enough. Which is why cities and states should be the arbiters of community standards, not D.C.-based federal bureaucrats and members of Congress from thousands of miles away.

On the state level, we got to watch the slippery slope at work. Once we surrendered our right to operate or patronize businesses without a fight, the slope got steep. Particularly in states and counties headed by progressive governors with a bias toward big-government solutions.

Some states locked down immediately and stayed locked down for months. Others tried to use the least restrictive means to accomplish the goal, allowing a broad range of businesses to voluntarily adapt to new conditions so they could continue operating. What started as fifteen days to stop the spread morphed into months of draconian measures to enforce inconsistent restrictions relying on contradictory science. The slippery slope at the state level began with elected officials—and sometimes appointed officials—taking the prerogative to dictate which businesses were essential and which were nonessential.

It sounded simple at first. Grocery stores are obviously essential. Indoor concerts are obviously not. But the slope quickly went downhill from there. The question of what is essential is a subjective one. Giving government the power to decide who must forcibly close and who can remain open gave government new power to pick winners and losers.

When Government Overreaches

The problem with one size fits all is that it doesn't. What is essential to one American may be superfluous to another. In a free country, we're allowed to hold different values on such questions. For someone who never attends church, church is nonessential. For someone like me who eschews alcohol, liquor is nonessential. For someone whose job is secure, like most of the people making decisions about what was essential, shutting down someone's livelihood is a small sacrifice when weighed against saving lives. Once again, where you stand depends on where you sit.

But individuals didn't get to make those decisions. Government did. In some cases, it was with a heavy hand. By outsourcing those decisions to people who, in many cases, did not share our values and priorities, we surrendered to government rights it had no authority to abridge. Now government would get to decide who was necessary and who wasn't; who could earn a living and who couldn't; whose life mattered and whose life didn't.

In Michigan, an elderly barber had his license suspended when he refused to stop giving haircuts. In Texas, a hairdresser was jailed for continuing to cut hair. In New Jersey, two gym owners were fined $130,000 for defying Governor Murphy's closure order after the state rejected their plan to open responsibly. In New York, Governor Cuomo suspended licenses of 132 bars, in part for serving alcohol without requiring people to order food. In New Orleans, the mayor signed an order allowing the city to suspend the sale of guns. In Wisconsin, police shut down a religious service in the middle of a sermon on Palm Sunday. Around the country, "nonessential" small businesses forced to close struggled to stay afloat as their customers flocked to big-box competitors who were considered essential. Some businesses were permitted to open provided they could prove social distancing and require masks. Others were given no such choice.

One step at a time, we slid toward an authoritarian future in which our rights are dictated by government. At first it was just fifteen days to stop the spread. Then it was just until we flattened the curve; just to keep from overwhelming the hospitals; just the nonessential businesses. Just until the death rate drops became just until the case rate disappears. Over time, the goalposts shifted, always requiring longer lockdowns. Fifteen days became five weeks and then five months. Once we flattened the curve, they told us we had to stay locked down because people were still dying. Once the field hospitals closed and the permanent hospitals had capacity, we needed to keep restrictions until the death rate dropped. Once the so-called nonessential businesses closed, the constitutionally protected activities—such as church, lockdown protests, and certain types of social media posts—also had to be shut down. Once the death rate dropped, we had to keep restrictions in place because case counts were still climbing.

Andrew Napolitano posed a prescient question in late May as some states began to slowly reopen. What good are constitutional rights if they are violated when Americans get sick? Napolitano, a former New Jersey judge, wrote, "Today, the fear of contagion gives government cover for its assaults on freedom and poses a question the government does not want to answer: If liberty can be taken away in times of crisis, then is it really liberty; or is it just a license, via a temporary government permission slip, subject to the whims of politicians in power?"

Once government learns its powers become unlimited in a crisis, the crises become unlimited. And in 2020, the worst pandemic in a hundred years was apparently not enough of a crisis to ensure progressive priorities would become law. There would need to be more. By the end of May, the virus appeared to be fading away. In many places the economy was opening back up. Summer was coming. And a new crisis was being born.

CHAPTER 6

CLENCHED FISTS

Race as Leverage

In light of the immediacy, urgency, and gravity of the public health crisis that gripped the world during the first half of 2020, it's impressive that the left was able to seize the spotlight beginning in early June for a new crisis—one that presumably existed during the entirety of the Obama administration, but suddenly and without warning became more urgent than a global pandemic. The brutal death of George Floyd on May 25, 2020, presented the left with an opportunity to capitalize on one of their top political priorities. Skeptics might call that priority "identity politics"—the notion that people could be divided against one another by their race, gender, or sexual orientation and would vote accordingly. Democrats might describe it as a deeply held desire to end racism, expand opportunities for a traditional underclass, and draw attention to concerns about targeted police brutality. If the goal were the latter, this was a perfect opportunity to unify a nation universally appalled by Floyd's death. Few have been willing to defend the actions of the white police officer who put a knee to Floyd's neck for nearly nine long minutes.

For a moment, we were all united. Everyone who saw that

early video was sickened by it. Not just black people. Not just leftists. Everyone. We all had questions.

But instead of embracing the chance to build upon that unity and develop lasting solutions, activists chose an approach guaranteed to divide us. They chose fearmongering. While there is certainly nothing wrong with questioning policies that lead to disastrous outcomes and looking for solutions, that isn't what happened. Disaster liberalism sees a building on fire and starts with nationalizing the fire alarm industry. And that's exactly what happened.

It soon became clear that these protests would be characterized by destruction—and the rioters didn't really care about preserving black lives or livelihoods. Ironically, the chaos ended up hurting the poor the most, since the rich were able to isolate themselves from the anarchy. Worst of all: we just talked about the chaos instead of the de facto pro-crime policies of the Democrats.

Given the choice between solving a long-standing problem and scoring political points, they chose to play politics. Instead of focusing on the race issue, leftists used the Floyd incident and the explosive response to it as a way to leverage unrelated policy priorities. Suddenly everything was racist—and the only solutions were leftist policy priorities ranging from climate change to Medicare-for-All. Their prescription for solving racism in America was the exact same prescription they offer in every other crisis—more government, more regulation, and more spending directed at left-leaning constituencies. It was a declaration of war—a clenched fist aimed at anyone who stood in their way. It was in many cases privileged liberals telling underprivileged America what was best for them. And what was best for them, in addition to a progressive policy agenda, apparently included the destruction of minority communities, the stoking of fear and anger, and the repudiation of law enforcement.

No doubt our criminal justice system could use some improvements and reforms. I know firsthand we have bipartisan support for such policies if we work together—because I did it as a member of Congress. Federal sentencing guidelines, correctional programs in our prison systems, and qualified immunity policies can be reformed or improved. The demands of disaster liberalism went far beyond reining in dirty cops or addressing excessive prison sentences. The Black Lives Matter movement is an explicitly Marxist organization with a goal of replacing the most successful economic and social systems in world history with systems that show a long record of abysmal failures.

As protests morphed into riots and riots morphed into widespread looting and vandalism during that first weekend in June 2020, the message that black lives matter was dwarfed by the agenda of Black Lives Matter. The huge gap between the sentiment and the political movement widened further.

Protests continually described as peaceful turned out not to be so peaceful. Protesters allegedly committed to ending police brutality turned out only to be against police, not so much against brutality. At times the movement seemed more focused on the grievances of criminals (of any color) than on the security of law-abiding Americans (of every color). During this time, any relatively recent murder of a black victim by a white perpetrator sparked intense scrutiny, media coverage, and backlash.

Unfortunately, the murder of black men, women, or children only drew attention if the perpetrator was white. The destruction of black-owned businesses was written off by protesters who assumed it would all be covered by insurance anyway. It often wasn't—not enough, anyway. Insurance payouts didn't come close to making businesses whole. In Minneapolis, for example, the cost of demolition alone frequently exceeded the payout from insurance, according to reporting by the *Minneapolis Star Tribune*. In many cases, their August 2020 reporting found the price of damage recovery exceeded the value of the property destroyed. Typical policies covered $25,000 to $50,000 in damages while bids for restoration costs were coming in at $200,000 to $300,000.

Critical supply chains into inner cities—the businesses upon which the homeless and disadvantaged depended for food, medicine, and health services—were destroyed without a second thought. More often than not, white liberals were egging it on. In fact, as it all unfolded on American screens, the angriest voices seemed to come from white people.

In Portland, where violent protests continued deep into the summer, Officer Jakhary Jackson described the racism he experienced from white protesters as a black officer. In a July 9 briefing, Jackson explained: "You are at a Black Lives Matter protest. You have more minorities on the police side than you have in a violent crowd. You have white people screaming at black officers, 'You have the biggest nose I've ever seen.'"

Jackson then went on to describe how his interactions with people of color during the protests were often productive and positive—until a white protester would inevitably interrupt to sow distrust.

"A lot of times, someone of color—black, Hispanic, Asian—will come up to the fence, and directly want to talk to me: 'Hey, what do you think about George Floyd? What do you think about what happened with the police?'"

Then he described how "someone white" would interrupt to say, "Eff the police" or "Don't talk to him." "I got to see folks that really do want change like the rest of us, that have been impacted by racism. And then I got to see those people get faded out by people who have no idea what racism is all about, that don't even know that the tactics they're using are the same tactics that were used against my people."

The real message of the riots did not seem to be the preservation of black lives, black businesses, or black communities. Indeed, these riots were better characterized by the destruction of those things. The idea that black lives should matter was little more than a pretext for what the left really wanted: political power. The top priority for protest leaders was Defund the Police, although there seemed to be some confusion about what that actually meant.

Many have tried to assure us that defunding the police does not mean literally defunding the police. PBS White House correspondent Yamiche Alcindor tweeted on June 8, "SOME NEEDED CONTEXT: Activists calling for defunding the police are not always calling for dismantling departments. In many cases, it means redirecting funds from police departments to other parts of society that help people like housing, education, and communities."

But New York congresswoman Alexandria Ocasio-Cortez pushed back. Her June 30 statement read unequivocally:

> Defunding police means defunding police. It does not mean budget tricks or funny math. It does not mean moving school police officers from the NYPD budget to the Department of Education's budget so that the exact same police remain in schools. It does not mean counting overtime cuts as cuts, even as NYPD ignores every attempt by City Council to curb overtime spending and overspends on overtime anyways. It does not mean hiring more police officers while cutting more than $800M from NYC schools. If these reports are accurate, then these proposed "cuts" to NYPD's budget are a disingenuous illusion. This is not a victory. The fight to defund policing continues.

Penalizing and punishing the police seemed to be the end, not just the means to another end. As for black lives, it didn't matter if the police were black, brown, gay, or transgender. These identity classes were never the priority. If anyone seemed to be a priority to these groups, it was the people committing crimes.

Sadly, those who will pay the highest price for the escalation of this crisis are the most vulnerable among us. As Democrat politicians like Portland mayor Ted Wheeler and Chicago mayor Lori Lightfoot excused the violence and railed against federal attempts to preserve the rule of law, it was the disadvantaged who were left without protection. The wealthy will find ways to protect themselves.

Lightfoot herself demonstrated this principle in August. Appearing on CBS's *Face the Nation*, Lightfoot claimed the "vast majority" of people protesting in Chicago were peaceful. One day earlier, twenty-four people were arrested and seventeen officers injured in protest-related conflicts. Days later, Lightfoot banned protesters on her own block, saying, "I have a right to make sure that my home is secure," and "I make no apologies whatsoever." Lightfoot has the entire Chicago PD at her disposal. Residents of her city cannot even purchase a weapon for self-defense without jumping through a maze of hoops that includes sixteen hours of instruction, a $150 application fee, a gun range test, and additional course work on gun safety. Lightfoot went to greater lengths to preserve her home block than to preserve Chicago's famed Magnificent Mile from looters.

When mayors and governors side with the mobs, inciting violence for political gain, kids get shot. Livelihoods get destroyed. Mentors and role models move to safer neighborhoods. And the vulnerable kids get left behind.

It's painfully obvious why those who live a criminal lifestyle would support an agenda to defund and decriminalize. But it's hard to imagine how such an agenda would benefit the lives of noncriminal black, brown, homeless, and disabled Americans who depend on police to come when a crime is committed. Indeed, those communities would eventually begin to push back.

Without the ability of police to use force in the face of danger, these communities faced the potential for rising crime rates, increased violence, capital flight as businesses shutter, and lack of access to basic services. High-crime areas don't create jobs. They don't offer stability or safety. They attract more criminals, devalue property, and scare away opportunity. Black lives did not matter in the face of the protests.

In many cities, they got what they wanted. As the protests continued, day after day, and week after week, cities governed by leftist politicians heeded the calls to defund police, to "end mass incarceration" by refusing to prosecute crimes both petty and violent. These tactics hardly solved the problem of racism—if anything, the destruction, looting, and vandalism reinforced existing racist stereotypes about disadvantaged populations. But for reasons that continue to mystify me, the left seemed to think these demonstrations of hate toward America and Americans were a political winner for them. Perhaps they did serve as the Democratic equivalent of "red meat for the base," but for many Americans the violence was off-putting.

Extended Hands and Clenched Fists

Announcing a historic peace deal in the Middle East between Israel and the United Arab Emirates (UAE) on August 13, 2020, President Trump turned to Treasury secretary Steven Mnuchin with a question. "Which is easier: dealing with Democrats or dealing with the Middle East?" Trump asked facetiously to laughter from the crowd. A practical Mnuchin prevaricated. "I'll be hopeful that we can get a deal with the Democrats," he said, smiling, to which Trump shot back, "The Middle East is more reasonable."

It wasn't much of an exaggeration. As Middle Eastern nations began to thaw in their relations toward Israel, hands were extended in an effort to seek peace. Other nations followed the UAE, committing to open embassies in Jerusalem and allowing commercial flights between nations long considered enemies.

It was back home in the U.S. where extended hands had turned to clenched fists. The symbol of the clenched fist has a long and storied history as the universal sign of revolution and rebellion. It's been used by radical groups ranging from communists to socialists and from labor unions to civil rights protesters.

During the Obama presidency, the Black Lives Matter movement started as a hashtag after the February 2012 murder in Florida of unarmed black teenager Trayvon Martin. It gained steam during the Ferguson, Missouri, race riots that resulted from alleged police brutality involving two other black men in 2014—Michael Brown in Ferguson and Eric Garner in Staten Island, New York.

The adopted logo featuring the image of the clenched fist has since become a potent symbol of the movement's violent resistance to our American system of government in general and to the rule of law in particular. Democrats nationwide have embraced the symbol and its accompanying policy objectives, which today seem to be not so much about racism as they are about decriminalizing crime and upending capitalism.

Ironically, in his first inaugural address, newly elected president Barack Obama in 2009 drew an interesting parallel using the symbolism of the clenched fist. Directing remarks to "the Muslim world" as it was then, Obama said,

> To those leaders around the globe who seek to sow conflict or blame their society's ills on the West—know that your people will judge you on what you can build, not what you destroy. To those who cling to power through corruption and deceit and the silencing of dissent, know that you are on the wrong side of history, but that we will extend a hand if you are willing to unclench your fist.

It was good counsel—counsel that I wish the former president would extend to his allies in the Black Lives Matter movement. The irony of Obama's statement is that more than a decade later, it characterizes the legacy of Barack Obama in America more than his legacy in the Muslim world.

It is Barack Obama's own party that seeks now to sow conflict, blame society's ills on the West, destroy rather than build, and offer a clenched fist in response to the extended hand. Though one could argue that the Obama administration extended a hand to the Muslim world (without even requiring them to unclench their fists), in 2020 his party personified the symbol of the clenched fist.

Indeed one of the most tangible symbols of the Obama legacy on race relations is not the extended hand, but the clenched fist. The first black president, who was supposed to bring racial harmony and social justice, presided over the birth of a movement whose adoption of the clenched fist is more than figurative. Now the chants and signs proclaiming "Death to America" were not coming from Middle Eastern terrorists, but from domestic terrorists aligned with the Democratic Party. In Rochester, New York, in September 2020, protesters literally carried "Death to America" signs while chanting threats of "Every city. Every town. Burn the precinct to the ground."

Liberal Lawlessness Flows from Years of Assaults on the Rule of Law

If the idea of decriminalizing crime sounds like an exaggeration, just look at the development of the progressive agenda since the Ferguson race riots of 2014. Long before the George Floyd murder, which became the pretext for the defund the police movement, efforts to lay the foundation for undermining the rule of law were under way in cities and counties across America. Whether or not undermining the rule of law was the purpose of these measures, it was almost certainly the predictable and logical outcome of them.

Led and promoted by a consortium of activists from Black Lives Matter and Antifa to mainstream nonprofits and media outlets, the effort to decriminalize crime has been most successful in deep blue communities. The agenda has included aggressive bail reform policies, the election of lenient prosecutors, the reclassification of felonies to misdemeanor crimes, and the establishment of sanctuary cities where criminals can safely hide out and reoffend with little fear of accountability. Whatever their intent, all of these policies deliver the same outcome: more crime.

When the rewards of committing a crime are not outweighed by the consequences, there is little incentive to behave lawfully. The result is always more crime. There are criminal justice reforms that are needed. I sponsored some of them as a member of Congress, together with colleagues from across the aisle. But today the progressive version of criminal justice reform goes far beyond addressing police brutality, promoting rehabilitation, or minimizing unjust sentences. This is the agenda for which the Black Lives Matter movement has been hijacked. Consider the outcomes of progressive governance thus far.

In New York, a bail reform movement sought to implement "cashless bail" policies that would ultimately release criminals onto the streets immediately following their arrest. The state's 2019 bail reform law was considered a big win for progressives, abolishing bail for numerous misdemeanor and nonviolent crimes. Billed as a compassionate way to minimize the devastating financial impacts of arrests on minority communities, the policy has not been so compassionate for the victims of its many repeat offenders.

Two months after the bill was implemented, the New York

City Police Department (NYPD) was feeling the impact. For the month of February 2020, they reported that major crimes rose 22.5 percent compared to 2019. There were 482 people who had been arrested for felony crimes who went on to commit 846 new crimes after their initial release without bail. Thirty-five percent of those new crimes, according to the NYPD, fell into seven major crime categories (murder, rape, robbery, felony assault, burglary, grand larceny, and grand larceny auto). That was just the first fifty-eight days after the cashless bail law went into effect. It represented nearly triple the number of crimes in those categories committed in 2019. Prosecutors declined to prosecute 803 of the new crimes. Democrats have pushed similar bail reform laws in communities across the country. Now add in the protests and race riots of 2020. Though police arrested more than 400 people caught looting and vandalizing New York City stores the weekend of June 1, most were released and were back out rioting the next day.

In California, Los Angeles County modified its bail schedule in light of the coronavirus risk, designating most crimes to require zero bail. What happened to Jose Enrique Esquivel is illustrative of how that worked out for vulnerable communities. Esquivel faced fourteen felony counts for stealing automobiles between March 30 and June 15. Each time he stole a car and was arrested, he was immediately released. Esquivel was first arrested on March 30. But subsequent arrests on April 28, May 8, two on May 14, May 20, May 23, May 27, June 6, June 8, June 13, and June 15 all resulted in his release. Los Angeles County sheriff's deputy Trina Schrader told the NBC affiliate in Los Angeles that Esquivel was "a prolific car thief who victimized vehicle owners with modest incomes," and "Suspect Esquivel showed little regard for the owners of these vehicles, who many times depended on these stolen vehicles as their sole means of transportation."

Fortunately, voters in California wisely rejected a ballot initiative in November 2020 that would have eliminated cash bail statewide, but that battle is not won. State lawmakers behind the effort have vowed to press on and Democrat governor Gavin Newsom had previously warned that he believed rejecting the measure would be "profoundly devastating." The battle over cashless bail will continue to be waged in states across the country in the coming years.

That's just one part of the overall progressive agenda to divorce choice from accountability and responsibility from consequence.

With funding from the foundations of progressive philanthropist George Soros and other leftist luminaries, anti-prosecution prosecutors have been recruited, promoted, and elected to lead a charge to release criminals rather than prosecute them.

In Philadelphia, Houston, Chicago, and other progressive urban centers, Democrats elected prosecutors running on a platform of "ending mass incarceration" who believe prosecuting property crimes is discriminatory and racist. Siding with criminals of color over the many victims of color, these prosecutors have presided over historic increases in criminal activity in their jurisdictions.

In California, Contra Costa district attorney Diana Becton, a Soros-funded prosecutor who considers herself a "gatekeeper" whose job is to "rectify past wrongs," has instituted new charging guidelines for looters. Before anyone can be charged with looting, Red State reports prosecutors are required to consider whether the theft offense was an emergency. In other words, did the looter need the products taken? They must consider whether the motivation for the theft was "financial gain or personal need."

In Philadelphia, Soros-funded candidate Larry Krasner was elected as district attorney in 2017. By 2019, the crime rate increased for the third year in a row, making it the deadliest year in a decade. In a time of unprecedented prosperity that included low unemployment and strong wage growth, we might expect crime rates to drop. But the first three months of 2020 saw a double-digit increase in crime over 2019. That was all before Black Lives Matter protesters turned portions of America's largest cities into burning hellscapes.

A month after the riots began, the *New York Times* in early July reported murders were up 23 percent in Philadelphia, 43 percent in Democrat-run Nashville, and 36 percent in deep blue New Orleans. Murders were up 24 percent in Chicago, where Soros-funded Cook County state's attorney Kim Foxx dismissed charges against thousands of protesters arrested by police. She then simultaneously launched an online process for protesters to report police misconduct. By August, Foxx had dismissed more than 25,000 felony cases—including murder, shootings, sex crimes, and attacks on police officers—during her tenure. The anti-accountability agenda doesn't stop there.

California in 2014 passed a referendum to downgrade property thefts worth less than $950 from felonies to misdemeanors. The purpose was ostensibly to reduce the load on the criminal justice system and reduce racial disparities. But the law has essentially legalized shoplifting in the state, with organized criminal groups hitting up one store after another, moving from city to city and never stealing more than $950 worth of merchandise per person in any one place. Voters got a chance to reverse that law in November 2020 but rejected it. This despite the fact that California's increase in violent crime rates exceeded the rest of the country and Los Angeles saw violent crime increase by 69.5 percent over seven years. That doesn't count any of the crime surge that followed the June 2020 BLM protests. Nevertheless, California's largely Democratic electorate voted to continue incentivizing property theft under $950.

If that's not enough, blue states have prided themselves on

their status as sanctuary states, where illegal immigrants jailed for violent crimes are released without notifying Immigration and Customs Enforcement (ICE) in an effort to prevent deportation. Instead, criminals are released to prey upon new victims. In Orange County, California, ICE reported in February 2020 that 411 of the 2,121 illegal immigrants released were later arrested again for committing additional crimes. These are new crimes that were preventable. More important, they create new victims whose lives can be forever changed by a violent crime.

A partner organization to Black Lives Matter, the Movement for Black Lives (M4BL) goes even further. They call for abolishing police and prisons. They demand "progressive restructuring of tax codes at the local, state and federal levels to ensure a radical and sustainable redistribution of wealth." They further demand "the retroactive decriminalization, immediate release and record expungement of all drug-related offenses and prostitution and reparations for the devastating impact of the 'war on drugs' and the criminalization of prostitution."

Whether by design or as an unintended consequence, the left's agenda to "end mass incarceration" has functioned as a pro-crime agenda that has been good for the guilty and catastrophic for the innocent. These policies sound compassionate in theory, but in practice, communities who elect the types of district attorneys George Soros likes to fund are seeing increasing crime rates and more victims. If the criminal class were to pool their resources and buy district attorneys to represent their interests, they could hardly expect better results than Democrats provided them during 2020.

In an effort to demonstrate just how harmonious their Defund the Police and End Mass Incarceration agendas could be, the left gave us a demonstration. In the spirit of 2020, both Seattle and Portland gave Americans a glimpse of what a police-free progressive utopia actually looks like.

CHAZ vs. the Republic

Among the most bizarre efforts to capitalize on the crisis of Black Lives Matter protests was the purported founding of a new nation on American soil. With the full cooperation of leftist Seattle city officials, protesters managed to take over a police precinct in Seattle, hijacking a six-block section of East Pine Street to set up their own progressive utopia. With Seattle mayor Jenny Durkan's blessing and Washington governor Jay Inslee's willingness to look the other way, a new Shangri-la was born on the streets of downtown Seattle.

At first, we were told CHAZ—the Capitol Hill Autonomous Zone—was intended to be a place of peace and tranquility. A police-free zone where people could grow their own food, display their art, partake of free food, and attend free teach-ins about the Black Lives Matter movement. Never mind the violent assaults and threats exchanged at Seattle's East Precinct that precipitated the abandonment of the precinct and the formation of the zone. Never mind the vandalism, the incendiary devices, the assaults on police, or the weapons permeating the area. CHAZ was going to show America just how much better life would be without those malevolent police officers disturbing everyone's peace.

One participant gushed dreamily to *Vox* about impromptu dodgeball games, people smoking weed in circles while others listened to a lecture over a megaphone about Marxism. They gathered to hear poetry, listen to music, and watch films. In theory, CHAZ was promoted as a beautiful idea—like rainbows. And unicorns. Riall Johnson of the Snohomish County NAACP told ABC News it was "an example of what things can look like without the police."

No doubt. And that was the problem.

CHAZ later changed the name to the Capitol Hill Organized

Protest (CHOP) in a bid for an acronym that better reflected the violent intent of the crowd. *Daily Caller* reporter Shelby Talcott tweeted about the name change, reporting the words of one speaker who shouted, "You are not here to be peaceful. You are here to disrupt. Does anybody know what happened to the people who did not get on board with the French Revolution?" To which the crowd responded, "CHOPPED!"

The change was apropos. CHOP would in fact be besieged with crime. Four shootings in ten days resulted in the murder of two black teenagers. Seattle would see a 525 percent increase in violent crime during the month of June compared to the same period in 2019, according to the text of Mayor Durkan's emergency order that ultimately dismantled the fledgling month-old nation. The order would detail reports of "narcotics use and violent crime, including rape, robbery, assault, and increased gang activity" inside the so-called autonomous zone. It would describe the pervasive presence of firearms and other weapons.

But in the halcyon early days of the autonomous zone, only Americans who seek out conservative media would get that side of the story. For everyone else in the progressive orbit, CHAZ was utopia. Left-wing media worked overtime to provide branding services for the movement, trying to maximize the number of references to "peaceful protests" in each news report. CNN's Oliver Darcy tweeted on June 11, writing, "If you've been getting your news from right-wing media, you probably think armed militant Antifa activists have seized a section of Seattle. But the Mayor's office tells me, 'City officials have not interacted with 'armed Antifa militants' at this site.'"

Indeed, leftist politicians at the state and local level were loath to acknowledge the violent origins of the zone, choosing instead to focus on the "street festival" environment and "block party atmosphere" that prevailed in the daytime. In response to Durkan's idealistic characterization of the zone, President Trump trolled CHAZ, tweeting on June 12, "Seattle Mayor says, about the anarchists takeover of her city, 'it is a Summer of Love.' These Liberal Dems don't have a clue. The terrorists burn and pillage our cities, and they think it is just wonderful, even the death. Must end this Seattle takeover now!"

Durkan fired back, writing, "Seattle is fine. Don't be so afraid of democracy."

It wasn't democracy Durkan needed to fear, but the fascism embodied by the very crowds she had emboldened. The progressive utopia of CHOP wasn't very interested in Durkan's rosy depictions of their cause. They wanted her to unilaterally meet their demands. When she didn't, or couldn't meet them fast enough for their liking, they enlisted a sympathetic Seattle City Council member to help them locate and converge on the mayor's home, bringing the summer of love right to her doorstep.

What were protesters demanding? They wanted Durkan to defund the police by 50 percent and "reinvest" the funds in community programs. They demanded an "investment" of $50 million into the black community. They wanted to end all contracts between the Seattle Police Department and Seattle schools. And they demanded all charges against protesters be dropped. In the bigger picture, they were demanding citizenship for any and all who come to the country illegally, reparation payments, and socialized medicine.

When all was said and done, CHOP organizers blamed outside forces for the nation's demise. Community leader Andre Taylor told CNN, "It is over because of the violence. I've told people here don't be focused on the location. CHOP is not a location. It's an idea." Retweeting the quote, commentator Ben Shapiro wrote, "This quote is EVERYTHING. CHAZ was always just a beautiful, beautiful idea. An idea that manifested as lawlessness, incompetence, brutality, and several shootings. But true CHAZ has never been tried!"

By the end of June, we got to see up close the difference between theory and practice. CHOP was dismantled, but residents and businesses within the former autonomous zone filed a lawsuit against the city for the very real damages they had suffered. Seattle police chief Carmen Best, the city's first black police chief, resigned after the far-left-dominated Seattle City Council voted to cut her staff by one hundred officers and reduce salaries for people who had been working overtime in dangerous conditions to quell the violence.

Seattle wasn't the only place being besieged by clenched fists. After forty-seven consecutive days of protests in Portland, Oregon, the Department of Homeland Security (DHS) sent federal law enforcement to do the job Portland mayor Ted Wheeler prohibited local police from doing. Though media coverage of the Portland protests had been scant, the opportunity to criticize the Trump administration suddenly made it newsworthy.

The so-called peaceful protests had, to that point, done $23 million worth of damage, according to a survey of local businesses. Protest organizers disputed the numbers, arguing the forced lockdowns were responsible for some of those losses. Regardless, the physical damage to Portland businesses, facilities, and parks was significant. DHS released a detailed timeline of damage done between May 28 and July 15, including extensive graffiti, broken windows, destruction of federal property, and removal of fences and barriers. They documented attempts to cause eye damage to officers using commercial-grade lasers, firebombing, throwing metal pipes, aiming aerial fireworks at buildings, and directing lasers at police helicopters. The "peaceful protesters" doxed law enforcement and got caught carrying pipe bombs, hammers, Tasers, and wrist rockets. Sounds more like domestic terrorism to me. Portland saw homicides increase, seeing a record fifteen murders in the month of July—the most in a single month for three decades. The city saw sixty-three shootings that month, compared to twenty-eight the previous July, according to police.

The cities run by Democratic mayors and policed by progressive prosecutors were covered in graffiti, filled with trash, and populated by emptied-out stores, some still charred from intentionally set blazes. Crime rates in these progressive utopias climbed. Data from the National Commission on COVID-19 and Criminal Justice documented the homicide and gun assault rates that began in late May following the death of George Floyd. Data compiled from more than fifteen cities revealed that homicides rose 35 percent during the month of June. Aggravated assaults rose 37 percent that month.

In New York City, where an estimated 450 businesses were vandalized and many of them looted, violence was on the rise and law and order in jeopardy. High-end shopping districts in Herald Square and Midtown Manhattan's Fifth Avenue and Madison Avenue were cleaned out. NYPD announced in July that the number of people victimized by gun violence the previous month—the month during which protests continued unabated—was up 130 percent over the prior year. Murders were up 30 percent, burglaries 118 percent, and auto thefts 51 percent citywide.

In Atlanta, where rioters had inexplicably targeted the CNN building, murders in the first half of 2020 doubled over the same period the previous year. From May 31 to June 20 alone, police investigated seventeen homicides and seventy-five shootings. Aggravated assaults were up 22 percent and burglaries rose 14 percent. Protesters did an estimated $10–15 million in damage in the Buckhead area of the city in early June.

Meanwhile, the pandemic raged on. It was easy to forget. Numbers had been declining and summer was on the way. With massive protests taking place across America, we could almost pretend the virus was gone. But it wasn't gone. A summer spike was coming, and then a much bigger fall spike. With it would come new calls for relief, more leverage to spend more money, and more demands for unrelated policy priorities. In the battle over emergency funding, Republicans had been largely successful in blocking the most extravagant items on Speaker Pelosi's wish list. But the war over coronavirus relief was far from over.

CHAPTER 7

THE CORONAVIRUS RELIEF HEIST

If you want to know what congressional leadership cares about most, you only need to look at what priorities seem to show up over and over again, in every appropriation, every must-pass bill, every negotiation. No matter what messaging the party publicly uses to define its goals, the real priorities show up in the legislative fine print.

In the case of coronavirus relief legislation, the aid needed to shore up a struggling economy was never the real priority—at least not for the Democrats. Relief was the leverage, the bargaining chip that Speaker Pelosi and Senate Minority Leader Chuck Schumer used to negotiate for what they really wanted.

Their top priorities during every stage of the negotiations were the same: tax relief for wealthy blue state donors, bailouts for reckless state governments and favored interest groups, economy-slowing Green New Deal provisions, relief for lawbreakers, and Democrat Party control of local elections. Having failed to pass these priorities on their merits through regular order, they now wanted to leverage the desperation of frightened Americans to force a power grab. If you read my previous book by that title, some of this will be familiar.

Nancy Pelosi gave away the game in a revealing April 2020 interview with ABC News' George Stephanopoulos. With three coronavirus relief packages already passed the previous month, House Democrats were gearing up for a battle over the next round of relief—what would later become known as the HEROES Act. Asked why Democrats wouldn't just pass a Paycheck Protection Program funding extension by unanimous consent, as many moderates in her own party were suggesting, Pelosi bristled. "Well, I don't know who's saying that," she told Stephanopoulos. "But I will say overwhelmingly, my caucus—and we're working closely with the Senate Democrats—know that we have an opportunity and an urgency to do something for our hospitals, our teachers, and firefighters, and the rest right now." She then added, "Let's get as much as we can for those who are helping to fight this fight so that we can soon open our economy."

It's a nice sentiment, but when Pelosi said she wanted to "get as much as we can," she was talking about what Democrats would negotiate *for*. The help for hospitals, teachers, and firefighters was what they would negotiate *with*. Those groups were just the leverage. Their aid was merely a vehicle Pelosi and Schumer could use to get what they actually wanted most. The real prize was something different altogether.

Democrats market themselves as the party of the poor and downtrodden, with an agenda to make sure the rich pay their fair share, that marginalized voices are heard, that government money is used to help people. That's not what their legislative priorities during the coronavirus relief negotiations suggested. In fact, it was nearly the opposite. To retain and cement their hold on power, congressional Democrats had a different set of priorities that had little to do with taxing the rich or helping the poor. In fact, this agenda seemed far more targeted at keeping donors happy, not voters. It's not about addressing COVID but creating welfare for the wealthy, rewarding reckless blue state spending, enforcing identity politics, and slipping environmentalist policies into ordinary life.

Welfare for the Wealthy

Taxing the rich is part of the Democratic brand. It's how blue states like California, New York, and Illinois pay for generous public employee pensions, benefits they offer to illegal immigrants, and expensive social programs. So how did Pelosi and Schumer end up making tax cuts for the wealthiest Americans their top ask in the negotiations over COVID-19 relief legislation? And why did so many in their party go along with it?

To find the answer, we have to take a closer look at tax policy—which is not anyone's favorite activity. But in this case, it can tell us a lot.

Some of America's wealthiest taxpayers congregate in the large coastal cities on the East and West Coasts, where taxing the rich has been in vogue for decades. In theory, states can only tax rich people so much before they start to flee to lower-tax states. But prior to the Trump presidency, they didn't need to. Taxpayers in high-tax states were protected from the real impact of those high taxes by writing off equivalent amounts from their federal taxes. By paying more at the state level, they got to pay less at the federal level. President Trump's Tax Cuts and Jobs Act of 2017 changed all of that, bringing very real pain to the wealthy donor class upon which Pelosi and Schumer depend.

Specifically, the so-called State and Local Tax (SALT) deduction allowed taxpayers who itemize deductions (primarily the wealthy) to deduct the amount they pay in state and local income tax (or sales tax—one or the other) plus all of their property tax from their federal taxes. The Joint Committee on Taxation estimates the value of that deduction prior to 2017 was about $100 billion a year.

Who benefited? Just six states, five of them blue states, claimed more than half the value of the deduction according to the Tax Foundation. Those states—California, New York, New Jersey, Illinois, Texas, and Pennsylvania—are among the most populous. For Chuck Schumer, the value of that tax break on his own 2015 taxes was $58,000, according to Americans for Tax Reform.

According to the Institute on Taxation and Economic Policy, 86 percent of the benefit of SALT deductions goes to the richest 5 percent of taxpayers. An astonishing 62 percent accrues to the richest 1 percent of taxpayers. Even the liberal Center for American Progress, a leftist research and advocacy organization, acknowledges a repeal would be regressive. Though Pelosi tried to sell the repeal as a policy to target middle-class households, Center for American Progress senior fellow Seth Hanlon told the *New York Times*, "The problem is, relatively few middle-class people claim SALT." Honestly—how many middle-class taxpayers pay more than $10,000 in state taxes?

The problem with the policy isn't just that it's regressive. It creates an incentive for states to raise taxes, knowing federal taxpayers will cushion the blow. The Tax Policy Center argues the deduction provides "an indirect federal subsidy to state and local governments by decreasing the net cost of nonfederal taxes to those who pay them." In other words, it shields wealthy taxpayers from feeling the true impact of high tax rates and shields states from the consequences that would otherwise result from such policies.

But with the passage of the Trump tax cuts, the curtain was pulled back, exposing wealthy taxpayers—a group that includes many high-dollar political donors—to the real cost of the big government and high taxes they ostensibly support. They hated it. So much, in fact, that they donated heavily to flip red seats blue. In the 2018 midterms, many of the seats taken by Democrats from Republicans were in these high-tax states.

Hence the commitment of Pelosi and Schumer to ensure repeal of the SALT caps would be a top priority. Schumer in July 2020 promised voters that if they would turn the Senate over to him in November, he would make tax cuts for wealthy blue state donors one of his top priorities. "I want to tell you this: If I become majority leader, one of the first things I will do is we will eliminate it forever," he said. "It will be dead, gone and buried."

It was an issue that came up repeatedly during the 116th Congress, but to no avail. On December 19, 2019, the day after the House voted to impeach President Trump, House Democrats passed a temporary repeal of SALT. The vote was almost along party lines—with a few Republicans from high-tax states joining Democrats. That repeal went nowhere in the Senate.

With each step of the coronavirus relief negotiations, Pelosi and Schumer sought to include this provision in the bills. In the HEROES Act, introduced in May 2020, Pelosi proposed not only repealing the cap, but making the repeal retroactive, allowing wealthy taxpayers to refile their 2018 and 2019 taxes for a big refund from the federal government.

Not many voters realized it, of course. They didn't call it "tax cuts for wealthy blue state donors." They called it "state and local tax relief." Voters were supposed to hear that and think they were pushing to plug state budgets decimated by lockdowns. And that was certainly part of the legislation. But not in the way voters may have been led to believe.

Rewarding Recklessness

Even state and local tax relief wasn't everything it appeared to be. We might have expected the negotiations over federal assistance to state governments to be simple. After all, both parties recognize the impact the lockdowns had on tax receipts. They showed a willingness to supply aid to states in the earliest iterations of the relief bills. But there was one problem: Republicans tied the early relief money to COVID-19. It couldn't be used to shore up preexisting budget shortfalls. Which is why so much of the aid remained unspent months after it was appropriated.

When Democrats talked about state and local assistance, they weren't just talking about helping plug shortfalls created by the lockdowns. That aid had already begun to be dispersed. They wanted aid without strings attached. States that had recklessly embraced unsustainable progressive agendas were facing the predictable consequences of their profligate spending. They saw the COVID-19 crisis as a pretext to solve problems decades in the making. Federal bailouts would obscure the unsustainable nature of their policies and reward the reckless at the expense of the responsible.

This priority was so critical to Democrats that they allowed the small business loan guarantee fund—the Paycheck Protection Program (PPP)—to run dry. Meanwhile, they debated concerns that a $250 billion funding infusion would not be paired with more aid for state and local governments. Despite the fact that the CARES Act had made available $150 billion for economic relief to states and much of that money remained unspent, Democratic leaders held out for more fungible bailouts. Their real priority was salvaging the fortunes of poorly funded pension programs.

With markets dropping and fluctuating throughout the

lockdown, state pension funds were feeling the heat. Not all of them were prepared to weather it. Illinois was the first state to come knocking on the federal government's door. As of April 2020, the state had nearly 110,000 public employees and retirees earning in excess of $100,000 a year. But for decades, the state hasn't been willing to set aside sufficient funds to pay the sky-high pension obligations that come with such benefits, putting Illinois on track to be the first state in history with a "junk" bond rating.

An Openthebooks.com analysis published at *Forbes* revealed the state's estimated $251 billion pension liability would equate to a $19,000 share for every man, woman, and child in the state. That's a higher number than the state estimate of $138 billion for the pension fund and another $54 billion for other post-employment benefits.

The analysis uncovered a government that pays a tree trimmer $106,663 a year; nurses at state corrections receiving $277,100 annually; 111 small-town managers earning more than $202,000—an amount that exceeds the annual earnings of every governor of all fifty states. They found 22,000 working educators earning six figures, and another 13,500 retired educators living on six-figure pensions. A junior college president was being paid $451,095 a year. In the city of Chicago, where the homicide rate routinely exceeds that of New York and Los Angeles combined, police officers earn up to $272,672 a year, with EMTs making up to $270,851.

So it came as no surprise when Democrat Illinois state senate president Don Harmon sent a letter to the Illinois congressional delegation in April seeking a $10 billion bailout directly intended for the state pension system. Harmon explained that pension obligations in Illinois crowd out funding of other services and programs in a normal year. "Clearly this will not be a normal year and that crowding out effect will be exacerbated by significant revenue losses," he stated. Harmon's solution is direct cash assistance from the federal government—that is, the taxpayers in states that don't pay their EMTs $270,000 a year.

While we can all be sympathetic to the pain Illinois has inflicted upon its citizens, a bailout only rewards the reckless spending. If federal taxpayers have to bail out Illinois, there is a long line of other reckless states who will step forward with their hands out.

Illinois's request was followed by another from New Jersey state senate president Stephen Sweeney, who asked for $500 billion in low-interest federal loans to be made available nationwide for pension bailouts. In Connecticut, taxpayers face a $60 billion unfunded pension liability. That's the amount lawmakers have put taxpayers on the hook to pay, but have not actually set aside.

Other states, including my home state of Utah, have made careful fiscal reforms to ensure pension liabilities can be covered. In Michigan, former Republican governor Rick Snyder signed trailblazing teacher pension reforms in 2017 that incentivized the state to fund pensions and rely on more realistic estimates of investment returns. Snyder's reforms also incentivized new teachers to choose a 401(k), requiring a greater degree of cost sharing for those who choose the hybrid pension option. The results thus far have been promising. But why should Michigan endure the fiscal pain of plugging those budget holes if Connecticut and Illinois can simply turn to federal taxpayers to solve the problem?

States aren't the only entities fighting for bailout money. Democrats consistently fought for funds to shore up the faltering U.S. Postal Service—an entity that enjoys massive competitive advantages against private sector mail delivery. With its vast infrastructure, it occupies some of the most desirable real estate in nearly every city and town in America—mortgage-free. The Postal Service struggles to compete for the same reason Illinois has a historic pension liability—it has caved to public sector unions, offering retirement benefits more generous than anything one can find in the private sector. Like Illinois, the Postal Service wants a bailout to cover fiscal problems that go back decades and bear no connection to the current crisis. Democrats want taxpayers—many of whom will never enjoy the richness of government benefits—to subsidize those generous union contracts.

Nancy Pelosi's original version of the CARES Act included a $25 billion no-strings-attached bailout for the U.S. Postal Service. That provision was stricken and replaced with a $10 billion loan guarantee after President Trump threatened to veto the whole relief package. Pelosi came back in the HEROES Act with another $25 billion request. This is a business that consistently loses money year in and year out. Without significant reforms, it's simply not a good investment. A 2018 task force study titled "United States Postal Service: A Sustainable Path Forward" included a series of important reforms to the USPS business model. The House Oversight Committee under Republican leadership pushed USPS to move forward with structural reforms. But when voters gave Democrats the House majority in 2019, the opportunity to make the USPS profitable was lost. Democrats hunkered down in support of the failed model, preferring to seek bailouts rather than fix the structural deficits that keep the USPS consistently in the red. Though the CARES Act provided $10 billion in loan guarantees for the USPS, that didn't stop Pelosi from coming back with new demands in the HEROES Act—yet another $10 billion in new lending authority. Once again, the long-term plan seems to be rewarding the reckless and penalizing the responsible.

Enforcing Identity Politics

One of the more baffling inclusions to the House version of the CARES Act was the diversity provisions Pelosi wanted to require of any corporation receiving government assistance. In the midst of a national emergency that was grinding the economy to a halt, Pelosi sought to force businesses to focus their attention not on saving jobs or staying afloat, but on identifying and cataloging the skin color of everyone around them. "Any corporation that receives federal aid related to COVID-19," the legislation read, "must maintain officials and budget dedicated to diversity and inclusion for no less than 5 years after disbursement of funds."

The bill required the oversight panel distributing aid funds to first collect diversity data from businesses and issue a report within a year of disbursement of the funds. Once companies took the money, they would be scrutinized by bureaucrats looking to analyze the gender, race, and ethnic identity for all employees. They would report on the number and dollar value invested with women- and minority-owned suppliers, forcing companies to choose suppliers on the basis of skin color rather than performance. Even the choice of bankers, attorneys, and asset managers would be evaluated. Government would scrutinize the makeup of corporate boards and justify their budgets for each position based on the skin color of the person appointed. The bill went so far as to order the Securities and Exchange Commission to set up an advisory board to study the results of the reporting and make recommendations. The Heritage Foundation's Mike Gonzalez pointed out the bill uses the words "diversity" and "diverse" sixty-three times and the word "inclusion" fourteen times. "This is not showing compassion for those in need," he wrote. "This is abusing the coronavirus emergency to reorder America."

The Green New Deal

Many leftists believe with religious fervor that without a massive restructuring of the U.S. economy the climate will kill us within ten to twelve years. That apocalyptic tenet of their faith leads them to believe climate change provisions must become law, come hell or high water. Coincidentally, hell and high water are also the natural results of failing to keep the commandments of the Green New Deal, according to leftist orthodoxy.

For the rest of us who believe in a more balanced approach to our stewardship of the land, some of the most baffling inclusions in the relief bills were the Green New Deal provisions. In a bill intended to spur economic activity, these provisions would inevitably slow the economy and handicap industries already fending off a deathblow from the virus.

The global airline industry was among the hardest hit by the pandemic, as borders closed, tourism came to a halt, and businesses eliminated or cut back on routine travel. Desperately in need of assistance, the industry found itself in the crosshairs of the left-wing climate agenda as Pelosi demanded punitive measures at a critical juncture of the lockdown. Senate Democrats pushed language forcing airlines to limit their carbon emissions—an expensive proposition even in the best of times. Pelosi requested a full offset of airline emissions by 2025. Her original CARES Act called for publication of greenhouse gas statistics for every flight. It also expanded a Federal Aviation Administration (FAA) program to get airports to create a "cash for clunkers"–type program like the one used by the Obama administration for automobiles, but this one would get rid of older airplanes. To encourage the production of "sustainable aviation fuels," Pelosi included in the coronavirus relief $1.2 billion in grants.

The House version of the HEROES Act, released in May,

included $50 million for "environmental justice grants" that allegedly investigate "the links between pollution exposure and the transmission and health outcomes of coronavirus in environmental justice communities." The words all seem to be linking the virus with the climate, but they don't actually make any sense.

Fortunately for Democrats, *Washington Post* columnist Sarah Kaplan came to the rescue to help create a nonexistent link between the proposed policies and the crisis at hand. Kaplan cited Penn State meteorologist Gregory Jenkins, who made the claim that racism is "inexorably" linked to climate change. It's all because of slavery—or something. Apparently, Jenkins believes the coastal communities where slaves settled are currently more at risk for rising oceans, hence climate becomes a race issue. Kaplan cites studies indicating climate impacts disproportionately hit communities of color to make the case that climate change is a racial emergency.

Wyoming senator John Barrasso, in a fiery speech on the Senate floor, questioned the relevance of climate provisions to the crisis at hand. "We're here trying to fight for the man and woman in the street in our hometowns and yet they're fighting for the Green New Deal," Barrasso said.

Pelosi wasn't successful getting her Green New Deal provisions into any of the relief legislation. Renewable energy interests cried foul when she was unable to insert aid they said they badly needed into the CARES Act or the HEROES Act. Instead, Pelosi shoehorned them and other climate provisions into HR 2—the Democrats' infrastructure bill. Known as the Moving Forward Act, the 2,300-page bill introduced in June 2020 was in theory a response to President Trump's calls for greater spending on roads, bridges, and infrastructure. But when the bill was unveiled, it was packed with Green New Deal provisions Pelosi couldn't sneak past Mitch McConnell's Senate in the coronavirus relief bills. Not surprisingly, it also called for a $25 billion postal bailout and $500 billion in Green New Deal measures.

Something for Everyone

Even a cursory look at the House versions of the CARES Act and the subsequent HEROES Act reveals they had something for everyone on the Democrats' Christmas list. It's not hard to see why. As the year 2020 opened, Pelosi had largely failed to fund her pet priorities.

With the House Speaker's party controlling only the U.S. House of Representatives and few in her caucus willing to compromise with Republicans, her power during the 116th Congress had been limited. She passed a handful of message bills in 2019—each loaded with provisions legislators refer to as "poison pills" because they are nonstarters to the other party and poison the bill against passage. They ensure the sponsors get points with the base for boldness but guarantee legislative failure by design.

Aside from those priority message bills, clearly designed to be dead on arrival in the Senate, Pelosi's House had little to show for their time in the majority beyond an ultimately unsuccessful impeachment effort that was forgotten within days of its conclusion. Her most vulnerable members would have little to run on in 2020. (And we now know they suffered the consequences.) Even if individual members could forge bipartisan compromises, House leadership under Pelosi was not in the business of bringing compromise bills to a vote.

The American people want results. Democrats had none to show.

But the desperate call in March 2020 for immediate infusions of aid to address the pandemic put Pelosi in the driver's seat.

Spending bills generally originate in the House. During a session in which spending bills had become virtually impossible to pass through the Senate, Pelosi was in control of a series of must-pass bills. Though Pelosi's House had spent precious little time or energy legislating in the time since she became Speaker, they suddenly had a hostage to boost their negotiating power.

Tasked with writing bills to provide needed economic aid to keep the economy afloat, the House came up with a series of three bills in March. The first two were small, relatively bipartisan, addressing only the most immediate needs. Though the administration had asked for just $2.5 billion at that stage, Democrats larded up the bill with $8.3 billion in spending. It passed easily because it largely funded bipartisan priorities such as vaccine development and public health. A second appropriation that month, for $104 billion, passed less than two weeks later. It funded additional COVID testing, an expansion of unemployment insurance, and sick leave. Again, it received broad support.

But then came part three—the CARES Act. Passed into law just a week and a half later, the monstrous $2.2 trillion legislation was the most expensive single bill in American history. It spent in one bill an amount equal to half of all spending the previous year. And it was only that small because Republicans in the U.S. Senate were able to strip out some of the most offensive provisions. *Ricochet*'s Tom Patterson called it "a massive transfer of assets from the private sector to the government, maybe the largest ever." The *Wall Street Journal*'s Kimberly Strassel noted, "A rough calculation suggests the single biggest recipient of taxpayer dollars in this legislation—far in excess of $600 billion—is government itself. This legislation may prove the biggest one-day expansion of government power ever."

Despite its $2 trillion price tag, the bill was skinny in comparison to Pelosi's original proposal, which received intense criticism even from friendly quarters like MSNBC. Correspondent Garrett Haake acknowledged on March 23 that Senate Democrats may have overestimated their leverage.

> There is a political danger of overreaching here. I think that's what you're seeing play out on the Senate floor where Democrats are being criticized for things like including cancellation of student debt, which you could argue is not a part of the coronavirus crisis. Things like you heard the speaker there talk about election security and vote by mail which is a very interesting issue for all of us covering the connection between the virus and electoral politics, but arguably not an urgent crisis in March.

Across the aisle, conservative publications were even more scathing. "What was striking here was the sheer piggishness of the grab," wrote *National Review*'s Dan McLaughlin. "The House Democrats' bill read less like an appropriation than like an entire presidential campaign platform, wedged into a bill that was supposed to pass a Senate and White House controlled by the opposite party."

In reality, the Pelosi-written CARES Act was dead on arrival in the Senate and the Oval Office. "There's no way I'm signing that deal," President Trump said. Thanks to Majority Leader Mitch McConnell's Senate, the CARES Act ultimately passed, but excluded some of the less germane policies on Pelosi's wish list: aid to state and local governments, cancellation of student debt, bailouts for Planned Parenthood, expensive Green New Deal provisions, federal mandates for vote-by-mail, mandates for corporate diversity, and improved union bargaining power. All of it was left on the cutting room floor, to rise again in Pelosi's next iteration of "relief" legislation.

Instead, the final version of the CARES Act prioritized the

things that, for better or worse, directly addressed the crisis: $1,200 checks to American taxpayers, as well as the establishment of the forgivable loan program called the Paycheck Protection Program to keep people on business payrolls through August.

But Pelosi and fellow Democrats would come back again and again, pushing hardest for policies that would help them secure and retain power. Again and again, we would see the same provisions show up in every must-pass bill: election reforms, bailouts, subsidies, and new regulatory regimes to enforce divisions based on race, gender, and sexual orientation. Each time, needed aid would be delayed.

Interviewed by CNN's Jake Tapper after the release of the CARES Act, Pelosi denied her bill was partisan and claimed it hardly represented a Democratic wish list. "It would be an endless amount of money if we put our wish list for the future in there," Pelosi said. "But that is not what the case is. Sometimes I get a little heat from my own folks who say, 'Why can't we do this in this bill?'"

That's hard to believe given the considerable length and cost of Pelosi's coronavirus wish list. But she is probably right. If Democrats could control every dollar of disposable income of every person in America, it likely wouldn't be enough to fund all of their ambitions.

In May, Pelosi introduced the 1,800-plus page Health and Economic Recovery Omnibus Emergency Solutions (HEROES) Act. The title was supposed to conjure images of first responders, teachers, and health care providers on the front lines of the coronavirus battle. But the fine print was all about slowing the economy, rewarding Democrat constituencies, and once again, influencing the election.

Economic relief seemed to be an afterthought. McConnell quickly noted that the $3 trillion stimulus bill used the word "cannabis" more than it used the word "job" or the word "hire." "Cannabis" appeared sixty-eight times, with provisions to protect banks that service marijuana businesses and to mandate research on minority- and women-owned marijuana companies.

The progressive wish list also included protections for illegal immigrants, federally mandated prisoner releases, and mandates for LGBT training. Acting Deputy Secretary of Homeland Security Ken Cuccinelli pointed out that the language of the bill created a deferred action program for anyone who worked in so-called essential industries. Buried deep in the bill was a provision instructing the secretary of homeland security to release illegal immigrants "unless the individual is a threat to public safety or national security." And if the illegal immigrant works in "essential critical infrastructure," they were not subject to deportation at all.

Constituencies who reliably donate to and vote for Democratic candidates were particularly richly rewarded. Not just the wealthy blue state donors who get tax relief from the SALT cap repeal, but unions, arts organizations, and journalists. Pelosi's initial bills called for pension fund relief for community newspapers, collective bargaining provisions to empower unions, and a $1 billion allocation to pay for "Obamaphones"—government-funded cell phones for low-income consumers. They called for $35 million for the Washington, D.C.–based Kennedy Center. The Senate compromised on that provision, agreeing to $25 million instead, after which the Kennedy Center promptly furloughed 60 percent of its administrative staff and suspended pay for its 700 part-time employees and musicians. Even student loan forgiveness made an appearance, with Pelosi calling for a minimum of $10,000 of debt forgiveness to each borrower. Nothing for the responsible borrowers who worked hard to pay off their own loans. They were out of luck. This benefit was strictly for those carrying a five-figure or higher balance.

While I'm sympathetic to the factors that have led students to be duped into borrowing prodigious amounts of money for degrees that don't always pay off, the coronavirus relief legislation was never the place to solve that problem.

But of all the provisions that showed up again and again in various relief bills, stand-alone bills, and appropriations bills, the most disturbing are the election provisions. Ostensibly designed to help improve voter turnout, these provisions were actually designed as a power grab to benefit Democratic candidates in the upcoming election cycles. That issue needs a chapter of its own.

CHAPTER 8

RIGGING ELECTIONS FOR A GENERATION

The deal was dead. Democrats and Republicans had been haggling over an August 2020 extension of coronavirus relief legislation that Democrats said was critical to getting Americans back on their feet. With presidential conventions around the corner, the two sides were not in a compromising mood. As negotiations broke down, House Majority Leader Steny Hoyer released House members to head home for August recess, not to return until September 14. That late return date would leave just thirteen working days for House members before the November elections, essentially guaranteeing little more would be accomplished by the 116th Congress. Coronavirus relief money probably wasn't coming.

But then something really big happened to change the trajectory. Bigger than the virus. Bigger than the economy. Bigger than the health and welfare of every American. So big that, Pelosi said, "lives, livelihoods and the life of our American Democracy are under threat from the President." This was such an existential threat that Pelosi would have to call Congress back from summer vacation to address it.

What could be so urgent? Mailboxes.

More specifically, an evidence-free conspiracy theory holding that President Trump was having mailboxes across the country removed in order to prevent people from voting by mail. Pelosi dutifully told the House they must return to "save the Post Office!" She had found the next crisis she could use to force liberal policies into being.

The Postal Service "Crisis"

The crisis started when pictures of the iconic blue USPS collection boxes went viral. One photo posted to Reddit showed a graveyard of the boxes stacked up behind a fence. It was reposted thousands of times. Twitter user @Tomaskenn used the photo in a tweet that read, "Photo taken in Wisconsin. This is happening right before our eyes. They are sabotaging USPS to sabotage vote-by-mail. This is massive voter suppression and part of their plan to steal the election." I know. We're not supposed to talk about the potential for election fraud or stealing elections. But this was back when they thought Republicans would be the ones to use the Postal Service to steal the 2020 election, so it was apparently okay back then.

In this case, a reverse image search found the image was not what it seemed. The collection boxes were indeed in Wisconsin—at a company called Hartford Finishing. An account tweeting as @UsHadrons exposed the hoax, writing, "They are there to be powder coated (refurbished), because that is what the good folks at Hartford Finishing do."

The same account reverse-image-searched two other photos of piled-up mailboxes circulating that weekend and found they were taken in 2009 and 2016, during the Obama administration.

Another viral image, posted by former NBA star Rex Chapman to nearly a million Twitter followers, showed locked mailboxes in Burbank, California. It read, "In your entire life have you ever seen a locked mailbox at the USPS? Now you have. A disgrace and immediate threat to American democracy. Shame on them. Shame on the GOP." One problem. The photo was from 2016—during the Obama administration. And the boxes were locked to prevent theft. Users could still drop mail (even ballots) into them, they just couldn't take mail (or ballots) out. This was the immediate threat to American democracy. Somehow these tweets went viral without a peep of objection from Facebook and Twitter, which would later censor references to election fraud that implicated Democrats.

With the photos going viral, the USPS conspiracy theories went into overdrive. The postmaster general was a Trump supporter and former Republican fund-raiser; therefore he must be colluding with Trump to steal the election! The USPS was getting rid of sorting machines ahead of the election to slow down the mail! Trump was trying to starve the agency of resources to ensure they couldn't deliver ballots. To be fair—that particular theory was based on claims the president actually made but didn't have the power to carry out.

"Alarmingly, Postmaster General [Louis] DeJoy has acted as an accomplice in the President's effort to cheat the election and manipulate the Postal Service to deny eligible voters access to the ballot in pursuit of his own re-election. #DontMessWithUSPS," wrote Pelosi in a tweet. She had successfully identified a crisis.

Or had she? Careful observers will note there were some obvious problems with this crisis. This wasn't a crisis, but a conspiracy theory.

First problem: Since when is the USPS a partisan arm of the Republican Party? Pelosi's scarcely credible concerns about partisan interference by the USPS assumed the left-leaning organization would intervene *on behalf of Republicans*—a preposterous notion given the long history of open endorsements and political contributions to Democrats by many postal unions. Pelosi's new crisis was more like a projection—signaling with these allegations what Democrats actually had planned. We saw that after the November elections, when frontline postal workers came forward to acknowledge they had been told, or were aware of, others being told to backdate late ballots to ensure they would be counted.

The second problem with Pelosi's postal conspiracy became apparent in September 2020, when Kentucky Republican Thomas Massie offered legislation to fix the problem and every Democrat on the House Oversight Committee voted no. Massie introduced an amendment that added serious criminal penalties to any postal employee "who would affix a fraudulent postmark on a ballot envelope." Massie warned that postal workers could manipulate postal equipment to submit ballots that were cast after Election Day in an election that remained undecided—which is exactly what some postal workers say happened. Democrats' refusal to even consider such a policy is at odds with Pelosi's strange fixation on postal service fraud.

In reality, there is no evidence DeJoy acted to influence the election or that the president influenced the decisions of the USPS. Efforts to make the entity more efficient were ideas that long predated DeJoy's tenure. They were part of a long-standing agenda to improve efficiency and reduce costs. The U.S. Postal Service operates independently and generates its own revenues. Though it does get occasional appropriations from Congress, its day-to-day operations are self-funded and self-governed. Trump is more than an arm's length away from how we vote, and neither the Postal Service nor state and local elections are under the thumb of his control.

Pelosi's fabricated postal conspiracy was further contradicted by an August 15 letter sent out to many states from USPS. The letter warned election officials that their deadlines for "requesting and casting mail-in ballots are incongruous with the Postal Service's delivery standards." In an effort to forestall problems with ballot delivery, the USPS was transparent about the potential for ballots to arrive late unless states adjusted their timelines. States had the time to do it. More important, they had the money. The elections are run by state and local governments, which received some $400 million in CARES Act funding to prepare for the unique pandemic election of 2020.

This effort to proactively forestall disaster in November was framed by Democrats as a partisan ploy to sabotage elections by a partisan postmaster actively slowing mail service to keep ballots from arriving in time. But the USPS itself explicitly denied allegations that the administration could slow mail service. "We are not slowing down election mail or any other mail," Marti Johnson with USPS told fact-checkers from *USA Today*. "Instead, we continue to employ a robust and proven process to ensure proper handling of all election mail consistent with our standards."

The Liberal Postal Unions Run the Show

Another reason it's ridiculous to claim President Trump was secretly manipulating the Postal Service is that the USPS is a deeply Democratic institution and has been for decades.

The House was called back to vote on funding in late August. They also voted to pass Representative Carolyn Maloney's "Delivering for America Act," which, had it become law, would have precluded the USPS from implementing any reforms or cost-cutting measures until the coronavirus crisis had passed. We were told that would prevent the election from being stolen.

Conveniently, the solution to the so-called election stealing aligned perfectly with the agenda of Democrats and postal unions: to prevent President Trump or his appointees from making any meaningful reforms before he leaves office, which they hoped would happen by November. Since my time in Congress and before, unions and Democrats have fought tooth and nail against any effort to reform the entity or make it more efficient. They prefer generous union contracts and large government subsidies to keep the USPS afloat. In fact, they demand contracts that eliminate any flexibility the agency may have to cut costs. Many American companies can keep themselves afloat during hard times by utilizing hiring freezes, layoffs, and other cost-cutting measures. But not the USPS. Their union contracts remove all such flexibility. Upon his appointment, DeJoy immediately recognized the $200 million he could save annually by cutting overtime, which USPS was using prodigiously to carry out its basic functions. Protecting that overtime pay is a longtime union objective. And because unions donate so heavily to Democrats, it's also a longtime Democrat objective. Postal unions and Democrats have for decades worked hand in hand.

So it's ironic that Maloney would describe the bill this way: "Our Postal Service should not become an instrument of partisan politics, but instead must be protected as a neutral, independent entity that focuses on one thing and one thing only—delivering the mail." Because political neutrality is not something postal unions are known for.

USPS unions have long been overtly partisan, openly endorsing Joe Biden for president, donating disproportionately to Democratic candidates, and even staffing Democratic campaigns. These are the people who handle our ballots in the mail. With a large mail-in election, they are a crucial part of the chain of custody of those ballots. Partisan political activity by the Postal Service is not unprecedented, but meddling on behalf of Republicans would be.

As allegations surfaced in late 2020 that post offices may have backdated late ballots in heavily Democratic cities of key swing states, it wasn't the first time we had heard allegations of tampering on behalf of Democrats. A 2017 government investigation determined that the USPS "improperly coordinated" with postal workers' unions supporting Hillary Clinton in 2016. The report from the Office of Special Counsel identified a long-standing practice of paying employees to take time off for union work that involved political campaigning, even as they continued to collect a paycheck from USPS. That meant postal employees were campaigning for Hillary Clinton on the USPS dime—a practice that had apparently been going on since the 1990s. This practice was done in violation of the Hatch Act, which precludes federal employees from directly supporting candidates. But this newest crisis had us believing Democrats feared the postal system had somehow been enlisted to steal the election for Donald Trump? What was really going on? Obviously the crisis didn't add up.

"Nancy Pelosi fabricated a crisis so she can make a money grab to funnel billions of dollars to the Postal Service because she needs it to pull off her No-ID Universal Mail-In Voting scheme this fall," tweeted Republican minority whip Steve Scalise of Louisiana, cutting right to the chase.

There was no scheme to have America's post offices rig the presidential race for Donald Trump. If anything, there were partisan postal employees allegedly willing to backdate ballots in an effort to support Joe Biden. Hopefully that issue will have been resolved by the time this book reaches readers, but it is a serious one that deserves every bit as much scrutiny as it would have been given had Pelosi raised it.

By August 2020, all of the talk was about postal conspiracies to help Republicans. Pelosi brought Congress back that month to vote on a strange solution, given the controversy—a $25 billion funding infusion to the organization Pelosi allegedly feared was going to help Donald Trump steal the election.

The playbook has become pretty predictable. There was no crisis. Just a viral hoax that had the potential to become a pretext for passing key elements of Pelosi's legislative agenda. Not just any key elements—election-related provisions that Pelosi was running out of time to pass. Had Pelosi truly believed Trump and his newly appointed postmaster general could use the USPS to influence the election, *she wouldn't have pushed to increase their funding.*

Pelosi's Real Objective

As House Oversight Committee chairman, I had jurisdiction over the U.S. Postal Service. I met with the postmaster, the many public employee unions, and the dedicated men and women who keep the system functioning. This pre-election "crisis" was not about them, or their budget, or their survival. In fact, the U.S. Postal Service had sufficient funds to continue normal operations into 2021. They had received funding infusions in previous relief bills that they hadn't even begun to use. The postmaster general said before the 2020 election there was ample capacity to deliver all election mail with or without a funding infusion from Congress.

So why was this Postal Service scandal such a high priority that Pelosi had to drag Congress back from summer vacations? Because it could be used as a pretext for what Pelosi really wanted: election reforms. Specifically, her party's relentless efforts to make local elections a federal affair over which Congress and the president could exert far more control.

Long before Patient Zero was ever infected with SARS-CoV-2,

Pelosi had made the nationalization of local elections a center-piece of her legislative agenda (such as it was). Readers can be forgiven if they didn't notice—Pelosi's House spent precious few days of their time in the majority actually marking up and passing legislation. Nearly every major committee was laser-focused on the impeachment of President Trump.

Nevertheless, the effort to wrest control of local elections away from the people, using legislation ironically titled the "For the People Act," was one of the few agenda items for which Pelosi found floor time. And not just once. Even after the bill passed the House, its component provisions continued to make appearances in must-pass legislation for budget appropriations. Though her repeated attempts to transform America's electoral process were dead on arrival in McConnell's Senate, help arrived in the form of the Chinese-imported novel coronavirus.

The resulting pandemic created the perfect pretext for Pelosi to try to remake the election process. Going to the polls in person would carry risk. Therefore, America must implement what House Oversight Committee ranking member Jim Jordan called "a grab bag of Democratic party favors."

The global health emergency enabled Democrats to push for changes that they perceived would advantage them at the polls and do it in the name of public safety. Along with mandatory vote-by-mail, Democratic priorities like nullifying state voter ID laws, prohibiting basic voter list maintenance, legalizing ballot harvesting, and suppressing campaign speech could be tacked on for good measure. Were it not for the Republican-controlled Senate, the 2020 election would have looked very different.

Under the guise of "election security," Pelosi would have partisan politicians dictate the rules of elections in every jurisdiction. She inserted election security grants that would fund local election offices and allow Democrats to attach strings to the funding. These provisions were not new. They could be found in multiple independent bills, stuffed into the September and December 2019 budget legislation, and again in multiple versions of the relief packages.

But in this moment of "crisis," Pelosi would hardly be honest about her aims. In fact, she would be warning *against* the very thing for which she had long been striving: a federal effort to dictate election processes. We know that was her priority because she told us so when she numbered her so-called election security measure H.R. 1. That bill number symbolically represents the top priority of a newly seated Congress. For Pelosi, that priority was election reform.

If you read my book *Power Grab*, you already know some things about the For the People Act. Now in 2020, we get to see just why we should be so grateful none of those provisions ever became law. Even as Pelosi warned of Trump trying to steal an election, he didn't have the power to do so—in part because her H.R. 1 never became law. The federal government does not run local elections. Not yet, anyway. But H.R. 1 was intended to bring elections under the control of the federal government, by centralizing elections, creating election security grants that tie beneficiaries closer to Washington, redistricting "reform," campaign finance reform that would dox donors, and public election financing. All of these efforts to nationalize and destabilize elections, however, are concealed with sly "election security" rhetoric.

Decoding "Election Security" Rhetoric

During the months the virus was dominating the news cycle, we frequently heard references to election security. It's a benign term that both sides support—in theory. But in practice, it's a loaded term. What voters hear and what leftist politicians mean are two completely different things. In fact, what Republicans mean and what Democrats mean by election security are as different as night and day.

In my experience, Republicans seek election security measures. Democrats seek secure-the-election measures. One side wants to ensure the votes are valid. The other side wants to ensure the votes are counted—valid or not.

When Republicans talk about election security, they mean the process of removing systemic vulnerabilities. They worry about the potential for voter fraud, recognizing that even one or two votes in every precinct can swing an election. When they introduce legislation at the state or federal level to address election security, they're talking about authenticating voter identities, removing dead people from voter lists, maintaining a secure chain of custody for ballots, and protecting political speech. Democrats not only oppose these measures—they view them as an effort to suppress votes. They see any security measure as a barrier to voting.

Imagine if we treated banking that way. Any effort to secure your account or ensure your identity would be seen as racist—and if your money gets stolen, oh well. At least we made it easy for everyone to participate in banking.

For Democrats, election security means something completely different. Determining what it means to them is challenging because what they say and what they do aren't the same. In many cases, they are diametrically opposite. The rhetoric almost sounds as if they are on the same page with Republicans. But many of the terms they use don't mean what voters think they mean. That's why we have to decode them.

First, let's look to the primary source—the bills themselves. On the day Nancy Pelosi became Speaker in January 2019, she introduced election reform as her top priority for the new

Congress. H.R. 1 was marketed as a way to drain the swamp. It in fact did the opposite.

Whether we're looking at H.R. 1 (the For the People Act), the subsequent SHIELD Act, the provisions Pelosi attempted to stuff into later must-pass legislation like the budget bills, or the election security measures she wanted put into the coronavirus relief bills, they all contain the same basic provisions, which are designed to give Democrats an advantage in elections. So what provisions are so important they merit inclusion in the top-priority bill of the session and get revisited again and again with each must-pass legislative vehicle? Let's take a look.

Centralized elections. Many of the provisions in these bills take power away from state and local officials and hand it over to Congress. The Democrats propose that the federal government should dictate who can vote. By that they mean felons who predominantly vote Democrat, those without identification who may or may not be legally eligible, and even people who just registered to vote today, whether they can prove their address or not. In states where the state constitution prohibits felons from voting, the bill would nullify state constitutions.

The Democrats' version of election security also dictates when people can vote by adding long early voting windows. We got a taste of the consequences of long early voting windows in the 2020 Democratic primaries, when three candidates dropped out within hours of the Super Tuesday vote, causing many early primary voters to feel their votes had been wasted. If states wish to reduce those voting windows, they would find that the power to do so has been stripped from them and given to Congress.

Democrats would dictate how people can vote, imposing a one-size-fits-all standard for mail-in and absentee voting. The way these provisions are written in the bills, voter identification laws would be nullified. Democrats would decide which ballots are eligible to be counted. Should national Democrats decide illegal-alien ballots benefit them at the polls, they could force states to accept them.

The bills also dictate how voter fraud can be handled. Under some provisions, even votes later proven to be fraudulent must be counted. They dictate how voter lists should be maintained, which is basically not at all. They include provisions that limit the ability of election officials to remove the names of people who have died or moved. Remember, they do this by precluding them from using the USPS National Change of Address database (NCOA) to identify voters who moved out of the jurisdiction. They further prohibit states from voluntarily participating in cross-check programs like the Interstate Voter Registration Crosscheck (IVRC) to identify voters registered in multiple states.

President Barack Obama, trying to mock suggestions by candidate Trump that the vote could ever be rigged, said in October 2016, "There is no serious person out there who would suggest somehow that you could even rig America's elections, in part because they're so decentralized, and the numbers of votes involved." In response to that election, Democrats proposed to destroy the guardrails that *Obama* identified as obstacles to rigging voting. They are taking the decentralized processes of more than three thousand counties and attempting to streamline them into one easy-to-hack, easy-to-manipulate process that Congress controls.

Election security grants: These grants, which were part of the budget bills in September and October 2019 as well as the coronavirus relief packages, provided federal funding for local election officials to upgrade equipment and pay vendors. But there's a catch. When you take the federal money, you have to use the federal vendors. Politicians in Washington now get to attach strings to the money.

In most cases, Democrats got only a fraction of the grants they sought. While Republicans controlled the White House and

Senate in 2020, we didn't see a lot of abuse. But these grants allow the majority party in Washington to dictate whether or not voter lists get maintained and cleaned up and how that is done, whether or not identification should be required to vote, and whether ballots can be handled by third-party political groups. This practice, called ballot harvesting, allows political operatives to collect ballots and submit them en masse. In some states, it has resulted in voters being harassed or intimidated to turn over their ballots, in ballots for the "wrong" candidate disappearing, and in bulk ballots suddenly being found and turned in after the deadline when results have already been announced, which changed the outcome of races in California House seats in 2018.

Redistricting reform. This misnomer is used to describe a process by which Democrats replace people who are accountable to voters with people who are appointed and cannot be held accountable at the ballot box. If those elected to represent the people dispute the new redistricting lines drawn by these appointed commissions, the dispute is decided and the maps drawn by a federal judge in faraway Washington, D.C., who may know little about the communities involved. Essentially, it transfers power from local legislative branches and gives it to the federal judiciary.

Campaign finance reform. Both H.R. 1 and the SHIELD Act contained transparency provisions to force the disclosure of donors to political charities and Super PACs. This is a provision that has the impact of chilling free speech. Imagine a world in which the only way for you to have a political voice is to make your name, address, and phone number available to the likes of Antifa. Today you can donate anonymously through a PAC or charity. But under these provisions, certain causes could be completely shut down by having their donors targeted by violent extremist groups. That was scary enough when the bill was introduced in 2019. But with the violent protests of the summer of 2020, these threats take on new urgency.

Antifa in particular has shown a brazen willingness to dox anyone they perceive to be guilty of wrongthink. After a flotilla of more than 1,800 boats paraded through Clearwater, Florida, in support of Donald Trump in August, militant Antifa protester Emily Gorcenski tweeted, "Does anyone have high quality images of the Trump Boat rally that show boat names or registration numbers so that I can start doxxing?" When the request went viral, Gorcenski trolled concerned Americans, bragging that she now lived in Germany. In response to tweets from Andy Ngo, a journalist who covers Antifa, one Twitter user wrote, "This is 'Crime Laundering' it's a technique used by Antifa to frustrate enforcement by exploiting the international nature of the Internet." Given the lengths to which violent extremist groups will go to punish wrongthink, Pelosi's attempt to close off anonymous political speech is disturbing.

Public election financing. Pelosi's reform agenda calls for taxpayers to fund political campaigns. That's right. H.R. 1 wasn't For the People—it was also For the Political Consultants who would see a windfall from the bill. This is their answer to injecting ethics back into politics. Candidates wouldn't have to fundraise, they can just play Mother-May-I with Congress. What could go wrong?

Now that we know what's in the bills Democrats consider to be "election security" measures, let's take a look at how they describe these measures.

Following her taking up the gavel, Speaker Pelosi held a January 4, 2019, press conference. She described H.R. 1 in terms to which few could object. It was, she said, "a historic reform package to restore the promise of our nation's democracy, end the culture of corruption in Washington, and reduce the role of money in politics to return the power back to the American people."

Let's decode that:

- "Historic reform package" = unconstitutional reform package. It gives to Congress powers reserved for the states.
- "Restore the promise of our nation's democracy" = ensure Democratic Party victories for a generation.
- "End the culture of corruption" = expose the identities of anyone who tries to fund our adversaries.
- "Reduce the role of money in politics" = limit free speech.

With no real widespread demand for the nationalization of local elections, Pelosi tried to market the bill as a way to stamp out corruption. In a November 2018 *Washington Post* opinion piece, Pelosi and bill sponsor Democrat John Sarbanes of Maryland described H.R. 1 as a way to "reduce the role of money in politics, to restore ethics and integrity to government, and to strengthen voting laws."

But based on what's actually in the bill, that doesn't mean what it sounds like it means.

- "Restore ethics and integrity to government" = let judges in Washington, D.C., draw the redistricting maps.
- "Strengthen voting laws" = introduce vulnerabilities to the voting system.

In tweets supporting the legislation, other Democratic lawmakers used similarly positive language. The late Elijah Cummings, Democrat of Maryland, then chairman of the House Oversight Committee, tweeted that the legislation would give the American people the power to more freely exercise their constitutional right to vote and strengthen accountability for executive branch officials—including the president. But if you look at what the bill actually does, it's like saying we got more people involved in the stock market by giving them easier access to your stock portfolio. When Cummings spoke about strengthening accountability for executive branch officials—something that hardly falls under the category of election security—he was referring to a provision in H.R. 1 that tried to force Donald Trump to release his tax returns.

Senate minority leader Chuck Schumer was pretty honest about what the bill would do. He tweeted in March 2019, "We're introducing the Senate companion to #HR1 because Democrats are committed to the fight to make ballot access easier." No kidding! With the measures included in this legislation, ballot access for foreign nationals, illegal aliens, violent felons, and dead voters would become much easier.

Even failed presidential candidate Hillary Clinton jumped on board, tweeting in March 2019, "Our democracy should work for everyone. House Democrats have passed a bill that would fix it through: Automatic voter registration-Early voting everywhere-Public election financing-An end to gerrymandering."

Let's decode:

- "Washington working for everyone" = Democrats in Congress controlling local elections.
- "Automatic voter registration" = felons, illegal immigrants, dead people, and ineligible voters automatically enrolled.
- "Early voting everywhere" = we're taking over your local election.
- "Public election financing" = you're paying for the nasty ad campaigns we're going to run in your state.

Oversight ranking member Jordan had a better title for the Democrats' bill: the "For the People Who Want Democrats to

Have a Permanent Majority Act." He called it "[a] laundry list of tired proposals designed to benefit the majority by tilting the playing field in their favor."

Though Democrats and their media proxies assure us that voter fraud is a myth, they love to talk about election security. They aren't talking about preventing voter fraud. They're talking about nationalizing elections. That's what election security means when Democrats use the term. They have spent a large chunk of their political capital since gaining the majority on this effort to take power from the people at the state and local level and give it to Congress, effectively nationalizing U.S. elections.

Universal Vote-by-Mail

Three months before the November election, with the spread of the virus slowing and the public becoming more comfortable using masks and social distancing to continue about their business, the need for all vote-by-mail elections was diminishing. Even Dr. Fauci was suggesting voting was safe. "If you go and wear a mask, if you observe the physical distancing, and don't have a crowded situation, there's no reason why you shouldn't be able to do that," he told *National Geographic* in August. Worried that in-person voting would suppress turnout of predominantly low-enthusiasm Biden voters, Pelosi proceeded to fan baseless postal conspiracy theories.

President Trump's trolling probably didn't help. In the belief that widespread mail voting would create opportunities for fraud, Trump admitted in a Fox Business Network interview in August that he objected to funding USPS because "that means you can't have universal mail-in voting because they're not equipped to have it." Of course, as we just discussed, the USPS was equipped, and had plenty of money to keep running well into 2021. They had no concerns about their ability to manage election mail.

But like cats chasing a laser pointer, Democrats rushed to set off alarms that Trump was trying to sabotage the election. From this crisis, Democrats would be able to prevent any reforms to the USPS, get the bailout money that would allow the agency to avoid reforms, and presumably accomplish one more thing that was important to Democratic leadership: provide a pretext to get one last bite at the election security reform apple.

Secure-the-Election Reforms

Ultimately, the case against centralizing voting is simple and intuitive. Would you trust Nancy Pelosi to determine the rules for your local election? Would a Democrat trust Donald Trump to do it? Or Mitch McConnell? Of course not. We're grateful our local election supervisor or county clerk has that responsibility. Someone who lives in our community, who has to take responsibility for his or her decisions, and who can be held accountable at the ballot box.

No one would trust that those with the most at stake in an election outcome could avoid the temptation to rig the game in their favor. They might come up with crazy rules that make no sense. For example, why would you make a law prohibiting election officials from removing the names of dead people or those who have moved from the voter rolls? Pelosi's election reforms went even further than that. They prohibited states from using the USPS National Change of Address Database to identify voters who have moved. They prohibited states from sharing multistate voter registration information to identify voters who are active in more than one jurisdiction.

These are the kinds of "reforms" we could expect if we allowed the federal politicians to take control of local elections. Measures to stack the deck in favor of one candidate or party are exactly what Pelosi said she was afraid Donald Trump would try. But he couldn't do it. Because the federal government does not get to run local elections. Yet.

But that hasn't stopped Speaker Pelosi from trying.

Protecting the Legitimacy of American Elections

Americans must stand up for local control of elections. We should support local governments in their efforts to upgrade equipment and embrace technologies that will keep voting secure. We don't need the federal government to dictate those decisions, those purchases, or the vendors that supply them. I would hope all of us would pay closer attention to the elections of those who manage elections—to their budgets, their processes, and their oversight. All of those things should be locally directed and transparently administered.

Nancy Pelosi may not like voter ID, but many states do. And they should have the authority to implement such measures. Sure, some states and counties will make decisions that give voters cause to question the validity of their elections. But correcting those mistakes is much easier at the local level than having to rely on a literal act of Congress to do it.

As for universal mail-in voting, there's no reason it can't be part of a free and fair election system. Though President Trump had some legitimate concerns about how all-mail elections were being implemented in some jurisdictions, it can be done securely. In my home county, we have embraced technology to ensure the vote is safe. Utah County uses a blockchain voting system to ensure a tamper-free digital record that voters can access, change, and confirm.

Republican Utah County clerk Amelia Powers Gardner has been at the forefront of the effort to promote universal vote-by-mail. According to Gardner, such systems provide a built-in incentive for local governments to better maintain voter lists. "Every ballot I send out costs me a dollar," she told me. "If I have dead people on my rolls, or if there are 20,000 people on my rolls that don't belong there, it costs me a minimum of $20,000. I have to update those rolls." Gardner does an NCOA update twice a year. That's something she would be prohibited from doing if Nancy Pelosi's "election security" reforms ever become law. In Gardner's view, it's better to send out all ballots by mail than just a handful as requested by voters. "When it's only 200 votes out of 200,000, you don't invest $150,000 on a machine that will match signatures for just 200 votes," she said. "But for 200,000 votes, you absolutely invest."

We have a lot of work to do as we try to adapt our voting systems to maintain a balance between security and convenience. If I had my way, everyone would vote on the same day with the same information. Maybe we extend it over a weekend. I'm certainly not opposed to changes to make voting more convenient, but ensuring the legitimacy of the election is important. It's not racist or classist or motivated by voter suppression.

Some states have made poor decisions about their elections, legalizing fraud-ridden measures like ballot harvesting. As more and more campaigns discover they can legally harass voters to hand over their ballots, I predict voters in those states will eventually push back. But even if they don't, I stand in support of local communities making these decisions—even when I think they get it wrong. If it doesn't work, they can easily lobby for change, because the people they need to lobby live right there in their community.

Desperate to pass her "election security" reforms, Pelosi will no doubt look for other crises she can leverage. Between the time I finish this book and the time it goes to print, I predict she will have already found one.

Learning to Let Crises Go to Waste

Crises have proven incredibly useful for advancing the dialogue, if not the agenda, in favor of progressive policies. And that was with the presidency in the hands of Donald Trump. I can only imagine what leverage could have been gained had real authoritarians wielded more power in 2020. It was a year of legitimate crises, leveraged to subvert normal checks and balances. No one can deny that a global pandemic provided an excuse for government to exercise powers normally withheld from it. While there is nothing more American than protesting, we shouldn't allow fear or intimidation to dictate our policies or our form of government.

Nonetheless, 2020 also gave us fabricated crises designed to influence elections, reward partisan constituencies, and bypass the Constitution. The implementation of lockdowns, the destruction of monuments, the post office hoax, and the vote-by-mail fiasco are precisely the kinds of crises used to manipulate the public into accepting unpopular and even unconstitutional changes. These efforts subverted constitutional rights, undermined the rule of law, threatened federalism, manipulated elections, and hurt the economic well-being of an entire nation. The emotional, financial, social, and mental costs of these crises are impossible to quantify. But real and lasting damage was done. As Americans come to recognize the contrived theatrics that surround crises both real and imagined, we can learn to tune out the noise and focus on the real priorities—maintaining our freedoms and liberties, preserving the rule of law, keeping elections free and fair, and demonstrating to the world why America is the most free and prosperous nation in the history of the world. The pandemic and protests weren't just a threat to our health and our pocketbooks, but to our fundamental rights.

CHAPTER 9

THE REAL GUN CRISIS

A pandemic might seem an unlikely crisis to leverage in the battle over gun rights. Typically the case against self-defense is made when there is a tragic mass shooting event, of which there are too many. It's a familiar debate, with the left focused on the ability of the shooter to access a weapon and the right defending the rights of potential victims to defend themselves from shooters who don't adhere to gun laws.

But if you think a pandemic cannot be leveraged in the battle to disarm Americans, think again. Disaster liberalism never lets a crisis go to waste.

Unfortunately for Democrats, the two biggest crises of 2020 would require them to embrace contradictory messages on public safety. On the one hand, Democratic governors would use the pandemic to claim gun sales were nonessential; that personal safety in a time of scarcity should be delegated to professional law enforcement. On the other hand, the riots would push Democrats to promote policies that defund police and release violent felons from prison. It was a recipe for pandemic-scale gun sales.

A New Bogeyman

As the nation of CHAZ was disbanding amid a rash of gun violence and the political backlash to weeks of violent protest began to set in, blaming white supremacists wasn't working. Americans could see with their own eyes in video posted across the internet who was behind the violence. Leftist media turned to another explanation for the violence: gun sales were up. It wasn't the rioting, the looting, the mobs of angry white liberals, the criminals released early from prisons over virus fears, or the release of protesters arrested for violent crimes. It was all those law-abiding people who had jumped through the many hoops in those liberal cities to legally own a gun for self-defense.

In Washington, D.C., where homicides were up 23 percent over 2019, Police Chief Peter Newsham blamed guns for the outbreak of violence. "I think we've talked about the increase in gun violence in our city for the last three years," he said. "It's really kind of troubling because if you look at violent crime in our city, every other category of violent crime, we've had significant progress in reducing those numbers across the city, and it's the gun violence that's the challenge I think we all need to tackle."

By mid-July, the city had already seen one hundred homicides—the highest rate in more than a decade. Meanwhile a police union survey showed 71 percent of cops in the city were considering leaving the force by late June. But local leaders were worried too many people might have the means of self-defense. No doubt that is the lesson blue cities would like to take from all of this violence. In their world, the answer to violent crime is to defund the police and disarm the law-abiding gun owners. What could go wrong?

Portland mayor Ted Wheeler, noting the uptick in homicides and violent crimes during the period of the nightly protests, blamed "an unprecedented escalation of gun violence in our city." Anyone watching coverage of the riots on TV or social media might rightly question the emphasis on gun violence when so much of what we were seeing in Portland was from various projectiles and incendiary devices. But Wheeler only wanted to talk about the gun violence. Suddenly, the racism that had displaced COVID as the crisis du jour was about to be supplanted by gun violence as the newest urgent excuse to violate the constitutional rights of American citizens. The solution, to this crisis and all others, would be more government, more spending, more regulation, and more usurpation of constitutional rights.

The Pandemic Impact on Gun Sales

The spike in gun sales that started early in the year was the trigger that brought Second Amendment rights under fire. Not just in red states. But across the country. As the virus advanced, millions of Americans caught the gun ownership bug, which spread prolifically along with the pandemic in the early months of 2020.

Long before looters, vandals, and angry mobs were left unchecked by permissive governors, Americans from right to left were discovering ways their Second Amendment rights might come in handy. The lockdowns alone resulted in a spike in gun sales. Along with the extra rolls of toilet paper, the food storage, and the medicine supply, people who had never seen the need to own a gun were lining up at the neighborhood gun store. As early as February and March, demand was spiking.

Staring down the barrel of economic catastrophe and a public health emergency, the nation's mayors and governors had a lot to worry about in March 2020. Given the complexity and scale of the meltdown they knew was coming, one might think it was all they could do to address the most critical issues. It was stunning to me how quickly leaders in blue state America pivoted to gun control as a solution to the public health crisis. It's not an obvious theater for the war over quarantine restrictions. But with newfound authority to make or break various types of businesses, going after gun stores was apparently an opportunity they couldn't resist.

As government suddenly found itself empowered to subjectively label businesses essential or nonessential, and to forcibly close those deemed nonessential, gun control advocates saw an opportunity to achieve a goal made impossible by recent court precedent: prohibiting the legal purchase of firearms. Governors and mayors began designating gun stores and shooting ranges as nonessential, despite the unambiguous "shall not infringe" language of the Second Amendment.

It took a series of lawsuits and guidance from the Trump administration on March 29, 2020, to begin reversing the unconstitutional actions in places like Massachusetts, Michigan, New Jersey, New Mexico, New York, and Washington State. The Cybersecurity and Infrastructure Security Agency ruled at the end of March that gun shops are considered "essential" businesses and should remain open during lockdowns. Though the guidance was not a mandate, it upped the stakes for governors considering forced gun store closures.

Gun control groups were livid with the administration's intervention. "While healthcare workers, lawmakers, and critical employees fight to save lives across America, the Trump administration is putting lives at risk by caving to the gun lobby during this crisis," said Shannon Watts, founder of Moms Demand Action for Gun Sense in America. A panic-inducing press release from the group read, "While NRA [National Rifle Association] board members have used the pandemic to further racist narratives, spread conspiracy theories, and dismiss the seriousness of coronavirus, the NRA has been fear mongering to sell guns."

No doubt the NRA appreciates the vote of confidence, but it's doubtful that persuasion by NRA board members or racism was the driving force behind record gun sales in March and April 2020, particularly when you consider where those spikes were happening and who was actually buying guns.

Though the U.S. doesn't collect data on the number of guns sold, it does report the number of background checks performed through the NICS (National Instant Criminal Background Check System) database. It's not a perfect measure—not all background checks are related to a gun sale and not all gun sales require a background check. But it still accurately detects trends. By that measure, firearm sales spiked in the months America lived in fear of the virus—even in blue states where voters don't necessarily subscribe to NRA talking points.

With a pandemic bearing down on America, the question of whether gun sales were an essential business was no longer theoretical. Americans were answering the question with their wallets. Politicians may have considered guns nonessential, but statistics show many Americans disagreed.

In February 2020, before the scale of the coming lockdown was known, the FBI's NICS responded to 2.8 million background check inquiries, the third-highest monthly total since 1998, when the system was created. It made headlines. But then came March. Though many states began shutting down businesses, gun sales climbed again. An astonishing 3.7 million background checks were reported, according to the FBI, far exceeding the previous single-month record of 3.3 million. April brought the highest numbers for a month of April since the system was established and the fourth-highest month on record. Sales were up 71 percent over the prior April.

In the first four months of 2020, the National Shooting Sports

Foundation (NSSF) estimated 6.5 million guns had been legally purchased—a 48 percent increase over the first four months of 2019. Sales climbed again in May, with gun sales nationally 80 percent higher than the same period a year earlier.

Then came the riots. With the ubiquity of violent protests during the month of June, the four-month-long gun sale spike had its own spike. The FBI did 3.9 million background checks in the month of June, with more than 2.39 million guns sold in a single month. In July, there were another 3.6 million checks. The NSSF estimated 1.8 million guns were sold in July alone—a 122 percent increase from the previous July. In 2019, just over 13 million guns were sold all year. In 2020, more than 12 million were sold in the first six months.

More surprising were the locations of the spikes. It wasn't just a red state phenomenon. Blue states were just as likely to see background check numbers jump. In an analysis of states with the biggest percentage jump and the biggest change in total number of background checks, Democratic strongholds ranked high, according to reporting by progressive outlet *Mother Jones*. Among the top ten by percentage change in background checks during those early months were Rhode Island, Michigan, Maryland, Colorado, and New York.

Some of the most liberal states and cities in America saw massive spikes. In June, following the riots, the state with the highest number of background checks was Illinois. New York saw a 121 percent spike in gun sales that month. In Hawaii, even before the anti-police protests, KITV spoke to 808 Gun Club owner Tom Tomimbang, who said he had seen a 400 percent increase in firearm sales in March 2020. "Not even during nine-eleven were people this concerned with purchasing a firearm. Our vendors don't have any inventory to sell us," he said. Most popular, he said, were nine-millimeter and twelve-gauge firearms and ammunition. "These are like defensive firearms. Most people buy them as a defensive type of weapon," he told KITV.

Minnesota Public Radio reported first-time gun sales in that state were fueling a surge in overall gun sales, with Minneapolis police reporting a 35 percent increase in permits sought through the end of March 2020, hitting a twenty-year high that month. Had Minnesotans known what was coming in May and June, they might have purchased more. Gun store owners reported wait times lasting three and four hours as Minnesotans flocked to buy guns following the riots. Oregon, California, even Virginia—where strict gun control measures were enacted during the crisis—saw gun sales spike.

As of April 2020, only 17 percent of Massachusetts residents owned a firearm, according to reporting from the *Boston Globe*. But of those who didn't, the newspaper reported one in seven wished they did. In March 2020, the state saw monthly background checks hit a seven-year high as the number of active licenses to own firearms grew by 22,000 in a three-month period.

Even the most liberal city in the nation, Washington, D.C., was not immune. The *Washington Post* reported in March that demand for handguns had spiked so sharply that the city's only dealer had become overwhelmed and stopped taking orders. This is a city so liberal that Hillary Clinton won 90.9 percent of the vote in the 2016 presidential race.

African American buyers accounted for the biggest increase in gun sales among any demographic group, according to research from NSSF. Black men and women reported a 58.2 percent increase in gun purchases during the first six months of 2020, according to NSSF research. "Bottom line is that there has never been a sustained surge in firearm sales quite like what we are in the midst of," NSSF director of research and marketing development Jim Curcuruto told *Yahoo News* in August.

Gun control advocates seemed baffled. Kris Brown, president of Brady—a nonprofit focused on ending gun violence— questioned the rationale for buying guns in the wake of the peaceful protests. "That this occurred during a month where we saw nationwide, peaceful demonstrations against police violence and gun violence inflicted on Black Americans and other people of color in this country cannot go overlooked," she said.

Perhaps she saw peaceful protests, but many Americans saw violent riots, overwhelmed or underutilized police, and destruction of property. They saw enough to believe the time had come to exercise those Second Amendment rights they had never before felt they needed.

Still, blue state governors and mayors persisted in using the crisis as an excuse to restrict gun rights. In Virginia, Governor Ralph Northam timed his signing of restrictive gun legislation on April 10, when Americans were locked down and protests would be less likely. Everytown for Gun Safety, a nonprofit founded by billionaire failed presidential hopeful Michael Bloomberg, pushed for mass closures of gun stores. The organization released its own analysis following the guidance from the Trump administration. It claimed, "States and localities act entirely within constitutional bounds when they determine that gun stores—or bookstores, or houses of worship, or marriage license bureaus—need to be temporarily closed."

Apparently, attorneys advising liberal mayors and governors disagreed. As pro-gun litigants began filing lawsuits to stop the closures, elected officials ultimately reversed course after consulting legal counsel. The clear language of the Constitution, together with current case law and precedent, ensured these were lawsuits they could not win. And they knew it.

As domestic violence calls increased during the shutdown, gun control groups sought to curtail the rights of women to purchase a gun for protection. Of course, that's not how they marketed it. They were focused solely on the potential for an abuser to turn a gun on a woman. But their solution of closing gun stores not only disarms abusers, it disarms law-abiding women, potential crime victims, and those who would otherwise be among the 500,000 to 3 million people who are estimated by CDC to use a gun defensively every year. In a 2013 unpublished study, a CDC-funded joint Institute of Medicine and National Research Council study concluded that "defensive use of guns by crime victims is a common occurrence," and that "[a]lmost all national survey estimates indicate that defensive gun uses by victims are at least as common as offensive uses by criminals." That same study, ordered by President Obama, found "consistently lower injury rates among gun-using crime victims compared with victims who used other self-protective strategies."

Despite the claims of Moms Demand Action, it's unlikely racism or "fearmongering" from the NRA was responsible for the spike in sales. As record-setting numbers were reported, news outlets set out to ask gun store owners what they saw driving sales during a pandemic.

After Minnesota's spike was reported, the Associated Press talked to St. Louis Park gun store owner Kory Krause, who told them, "In the event the outbreak gets worse and civil unrest breaks out, wanting to protect their family and their stockpile is really the vibe we're getting from people."

The *Washington Post* spoke to Dave Fullarton, who helps customers in a Maryland industrial park, to find out what was driving customers to buy a gun. "There's a lot who haven't ever thought about it," he said. "But now they've started considering: What if the unthinkable happens? They're stocking up on food and water and paper towels, and they're realizing they have to protect what they have in case of a societal collapse."

In Missouri, gun store owner Larry Wayland told the *Missourian* newspaper that most gun buyers seemed to be first-time customers. "They were just concerned that they might have to take responsibility for their personal safety and protection," he said, unknowingly foreshadowing events that would play out just a few months later in nearby St. Louis.

Even if we were only dealing with a pandemic, these were legitimate concerns. When one considers that the vaunted NYPD at one point saw 5,324 uniformed officers out sick, with 4,000 having tested positive for the virus, depending on police for safety and security was becoming a risky bet. It would soon become riskier. During that same time frame in mid-April 2020, twenty-nine NYPD personnel had reportedly died from COVID-19. That was a threat. But a few months later, the risks of depending on the NYPD for defense became even more clear as the force experienced $1 million in damaged and disabled vehicles, saw Democratic leaders cut $1 billion from its budget, and more than 1,500 officers filed for retirement—a 50 percent increase. Can New Yorkers be blamed for seeking to ensure their own self-defense?

As May turned to June, the possibility that Americans would have to take responsibility for their own safety became even more real.

Gun Sales and Politics

Conventional wisdom suggests that demand for guns is driven by two things: mass shootings and fear of suppression. Following the Sandy Hook shooting in 2012, the terrorist attack in San Bernardino in 2015, and the Orlando night club shooting in 2016, Americans stocked up on guns in record numbers.

But it didn't happen after the Las Vegas massacre in 2017 or the 2018 Parkland shooting in Florida. The difference may be politics. An analysis by *Vox* suggests fear of suppression may be the biggest factor that drives up gun sales. In 2017 and 2018, Donald Trump was president. "Our best guess as to what's happening: Gun enthusiasts don't feel the Republican-controlled White House and Congress will do anything to prevent them from buying the guns they want," *Vox* concluded.

By contrast, when Barack Obama became the forty-fourth president, within a month of his taking office he sent signals indicating gun owners should be fearful. He fundamentally changed the way ammunition was recycled within the Department of Defense. Imagine how many millions of rounds the Pentagon will use on an annual basis.

Ironically, the Obama/Biden administration sought to get rid of a recycling program as one of their first actions. I was elected to Congress at the same time Barack Obama was elected. As a new freshman in the House of Representatives, this is one of the first issues I dove into.

The spent brass from a fired round used to be recycled and used as the base of supply for ammunition for the military and American consumers. Georgia Arms, for instance, would buy roughly thirty thousand pounds of brass casings at a time. These were one-time used casings they could recycle into new ammunition. But the new administration was no longer going to allow these sales. Rather, the Department of Defense was going to spend new money to shred the brass and sell it as scrap metal to China. In his first thirty days in office, why would President Obama prioritize this?

Law-abiding American gun enthusiasts immediately saw the new president was going to make access to guns and ammunition very difficult and more expensive. Immediately there was a run on ammunition. On top of that, you had operations like Fast and Furious, in which the Bureau of Alcohol, Tobacco, Firearms and Explosives (ATF) deliberately sold weapons to drug cartels, which added to the narrative that Obama/Biden were going to do everything they could to make gun and ammunition sales difficult.

One of the unproven theories presenting itself from the Fast

and Furious operation was a concern that when the ATF know-
ingly and willingly put nearly two thousand weapons, mostly
AK-47s, into the hands of the drug cartels, there would be a natural consequence of increased gun violence. Many thought that,
due to increased gun violence, the Democrats would be in a better political position to enact new gun control legislation.

True or not, the perception and backlash was real enough to
make President Obama the number one gun salesman in America. Guns and ammunition sales of all types were reaching new
record heights. For years .22-caliber rounds were in scarce supply as demand skyrocketed. Yet they are some of the most popular and least expensive bullets on the market. You used to be
able to go to Wal-Mart or a local retailer and buy thousands of
rounds, but the sales were so brisk these retailers were almost
immediately sold out.

When Donald Trump became the forty-fifth president of the
United States, the same gun enthusiasts were not purchasing as
much as they were under the former president. President Trump
had signaled he was pro–Second Amendment and his margin of
victory against Secretary Hillary Clinton was certainly boosted
by people whose primary issue is the Second Amendment. With
Trump in charge, there was no immediate threat.

That is, until COVID-19 happened. That's when gun sales
began to spike. People sensed a threat and responded by exercising their rights. Had they been able to see into the future, gun
purchasers would have learned they were right about the threat,
just not about its source. It wouldn't be COVID-19 that drove
crime rates up and made American cities unsafe. It would be the
policies of Democrat mayors and governors who refused to quell
the rioting they believed was politically beneficial to their party
and the upcoming election.

For mayors and governors who religiously preached that
gun sales drove gun violence, the demands of people wanting to

protect themselves were not to be tolerated. Despite firm case law and clear constitutional protections, efforts to undermine gun rights went into overdrive.

In Jackson, Mississippi, Democratic mayor Chokwe Antar Lumumba signed an April 2020 executive order banning open carry during the city's stay-at-home order. Lumumba pointed to the shooting deaths of two children as justification for keeping law-abiding gun owners from defending themselves. The move was met with a federal lawsuit by Republican state lawmaker Dana Criswell alleging Lumumba "exploited the present public health crisis" to infringe on a citizen's right to self-defense. In a statement, Criswell told the *Jackson Free Press*, "The mayor's attempt to disarm me and deny me the ability of self-defense puts me and my family in danger anytime we are in Jackson."

In Los Angeles County, where 1,700 inmates were released from county jails in response to the coronavirus outbreak despite zero positive tests for the virus, Sheriff Alex Villanueva declared gun stores nonessential. A suit filed by the National Rifle Association and other Second Amendment groups alleged, "Firearm and ammunition retailers arguably provide the most essential business function possible by enabling Californians to lawfully defend themselves, their loved ones and their property."

The most restrictive orders came from governors in five states who ordered gun stores to close statewide. In Washington State, Massachusetts, New Mexico, Michigan, and New York, gun stores were closed, but in some states, they were still running background checks on the tsunami of prospective buyers. In Washington State, *USA Today* reported background checks in April were up 45 percent over the previous year, despite store showrooms being closed. In New Mexico, they were up 15 percent.

After the nonbinding guidance from the Trump administration was released in late March, many gun stores were emboldened to defy shutdown orders, shifting business online or taking appointments with customers one-on-one. Meanwhile, Second Amendment proponents took to the courts.

In New Mexico, the NRA sued Democratic governor Michelle Lujan Grisham after she closed gun shops and shooting ranges. Meanwhile, the state threatened to fine gun shops for defying the public health order. Local broadcast station KRQE reported one gun store owner was levied a $60,000 fine—$5,000 per day—for keeping his store open.

"What they tell you is that you're in violation of the Department of Health code," said Diane Rowe, who owns Papas Pawns and Gun. "Well, I'm not because I'm doing the same precautions that Walmart and Smith's and the rest of them are doing."

In Massachusetts, gun shop owners brought suit against Republican governor Charlie Baker for violating their rights with an April 1 closure order. Initially Baker designated gun stores essential, but changed the designation hours later. Lawyer Andrew J. Couture, who filed the suit, told the *Worcester Telegram* they weren't even permitted to hold firearms safety classes online. "How can you get the virus by printing a certificate from a class you took online?" he asked. Couture said gun store owners asked to be able to sell guns by appointment. The state denied the request.

In New Jersey, where Governor Phil Murphy reversed the original nonessential designation for gun retailers after being threatened with lawsuits, outdoor gun ranges remained closed. In an April 29 order, the governor permitted some outdoor recreation, but did not include outdoor gun ranges. The Association of New Jersey Rifle & Pistol Clubs sued, arguing that if golf courses can be open, gun ranges should be, too.

According to the lawsuit, "[Murphy's order] effectively bans the protected Second Amendment activity of training and building proficiency with firearms at the precise moment when the right to keep and bear arms is most essential. The citizens of New Jersey face unprecedented social disruption due to the COVID-19 emergency." With police departments stretched thin and unprecedented numbers of inmates being released onto the streets, the lawsuit says, "public acts of lawlessness are becoming increasingly common."

Ultimately, case law and constitutional guarantees will win the day. Both legal precedent and the clear text of the law recognize the right to own firearms for self-defense. But make no mistake, this is a right that will never be safe. There will always be those who abuse guns. And when they do, there will be those who advocate for the banning of weapons. But as long as there are people who would abuse weapons, there must be a right to defend against such people.

Selective Outrage

Just as the protests and riots exposed the political agenda of public health officials, they also exposed the sham of gun control policies. Portland mayor Ted Wheeler wrings his hands about "gun violence" when homicides go up even as he ties the hands of local police to stop mob violence in his city. The same people who pass laws to charge and arrest lawful gun owners who carry their guns in public, who would have police enforce those laws against nonviolent crimes, now rail against overcriminalization and mass incarceration. The same people raising the alarm about the danger of school shootings are supporting a movement that pulls trained police officers out of public schools. The same elected officials telling us to leave armed defense to the police are the very people pushing to cut funding to police.

The premise of gun control has always been that we should

outsource our security to trained police, who know how to use their guns. But now those same politicians want to cut back on police presence, reduce response times, and send social workers to defend us.

With one exception.

When it comes to the enforcement of gun restrictions, the story changes. In a 2019 analysis of a gun court in Brooklyn, New York, *Slate*'s Emily Bazelon described what she saw. Gun courts were established by New York City mayor Bill de Blasio in 2016 to fast-track people to prison who carry guns without the state's permission. Bazelon explained:

> I thought I'd find horrific stories of gun violence and hardened evildoers, like de Blasio said. Instead, over many months of my reporting, I found hundreds of teenagers and young people, almost all of them black, being marched to prison not for firing a gun, or even pointing one, but for having one. Many of them had minimal criminal records. To be precise, when I went through 200 case files, I found that 70 percent of the defendants in gun court had no previous felony convictions.

Isn't this precisely the kind of racism Black Lives Matter protesters claim to be fighting?

The hypocrisy shows up again when we consider the kinds of "good cause" requirements pushed by gun control groups. Cam Edwards, in a sharp analysis for Bearingarms.com, explained how those laws are written to work.

> Gun control groups are uniformly in favor of "good cause" requirements for a concealed carry license, and support broad discretionary authority for police to deny carry licenses to as many individuals as possible. If policing is an inherently racist institution, then what does it say about gun control groups

that they want to empower the police to decide which members of the community get to exercise their Second Amendment rights?

It's not just about racism. Or gun violence. Those things may matter to the people showing up for the protests, but they become a means to another end once negotiations begin. At the end of the day, gun violence is just one more crisis that can be used to promote the same tired solutions—more government, more spending, more regulation. The fight is about power and control—specifically consolidating more power in the hands of a strong central government—the very thing the Founders designed our system to counteract. For the left, there is a near-religious faith in government to solve all the problems. But doing so requires reining in constitutional impediments to the progressive agenda, of which the right to bear arms is just one.

CHAPTER 10

A LOCKDOWN ON FAITH

Within a few days after the CDC issued its March 28, 2020, request that residents of the New York metropolitan area curtail nonessential travel, Mayor Bill de Blasio made a startling pronouncement:

> Everyone has been instructed that if they see worship services going on, they will go to the officials of that congregation and inform them that they need to stop the services and disperse. . . . If that does not happen, they will take additional action up to the point of fines and potentially closing the building *permanently*. Again, that will begin this weekend.

Permanently? De Blasio threatened to close churches *permanently*? He suggested no due process. Just an edict, as if he were some kind of king. But this was America, not eighteenth-century England. New York was no longer the land of royalists and Tories. There were no kings there. De Blasio lacked the power to permanently close a church or to seize a building rightfully owned by one.

But just what are the limits of authority on elected officials in the face of a health crisis? Obviously, lives were on the line. Public health was at risk. Yet religious exercise, like free speech and free assembly, is a protected right. Religious rights enjoy greater constitutional protection than the right to grocery shop, pursue home improvement projects, or buy liquor—all of which enjoyed universal protection during the pandemic. Religion is vital to public life. But the problem is, to liberal statists, religion poses a threat. Religious groups do not wield the same cultural power as protesters, which was revealed beyond all doubt when the Nanny State felt free to trample the rights of Americans of faith, while cheerfully enabling political antiracist protests.

Why Religion Remains a Threat

Even in the best of times, these are thorny questions. But 2020 was a time of real crisis, being a heated presidential election year, the beginning of a deadly pandemic, and the kindling of violent riots across the nation. Unfortunately, that made it ripe for political opportunists with a bone to pick with religious Americans.

The First Amendment, and specifically its religion clause, is an impediment to those who seek to consolidate vast reserves of power in a single entity. Everywhere we see totalitarianism and dictatorship going off the rails, we can trace a path back to suppression of speech, religion, assembly, and the press. Outside the U.S., finding examples of religious suppression is not difficult. In China, minority Muslim Uighurs are persecuted and oppressed, their men used for forced labor and their women raped and forcibly sterilized. Practitioners of Falun Gong are reportedly used as unwilling organ donors, their lives sacrificed for the crime of following the wrong religious movement. In July, China reportedly threatened Christian welfare recipients with the loss of government support unless they removed religious symbols and replaced them with images of current or past communist leaders. In nations from Nigeria to India and from Pakistan to North Korea, governments target Christians or look the other way as persecutions rage against them. The Iranian government targets the Baha'is; the Pakistanis employ forced conversions of Hindus, Sikhs, and Christians. The Russian government oppresses religious minorities of all stripes.

In the U.S., both the left and the right support the First Amendment—in theory. But in practice, many leftists are virulently antireligion, clinging to the old Karl Marx adage that "religion is the sigh of the oppressed creature" and "the opium of the people." As Democratic orthodoxy has marched leftward, it has come into conflict with religious beliefs about marriage, gender, sexual orientation, family structure, and perhaps most notably, principles of choice and accountability. Given these conflicts, the opportunity to use a public health crisis for political advantage—as a means to hit back at religious Americans—was too good to pass up.

It wasn't enough for Democratic politicians to make broad restrictions on gatherings irrespective of whether they were religious. Elected officials took religious prohibitions even *further*, targeting restrictions specifically to religious practice and stretching constitutional limits to the point that government restrictions would have to be overruled by the courts.

Forced Compliance

The vast majority of churches in the weeks following the economic lockdown would voluntarily comply with a request to close temporarily. The sign in front of Rhode Island's Edgewood

Congregational Church read, "Services cancelled. God making house calls."

Some churches would soon respond with innovative new ways to safely conduct services—some online, others in cars. Leaders of my own faith had already developed a home-based curriculum to assist families in teaching Sunday school in the home.

President Trump publicly acknowledged the need to mitigate risk, telling the nation in early April, "My biggest disappointment is that churches can't meet in a time of need." He didn't encourage people to worship publicly. He didn't imply the use of force to prohibit them from doing so. He simply acknowledged their disappointment, trusting that they would act responsibly.

Liberty comes with both rights and responsibilities. When both are exercised, force is not necessary. President Trump seemed to understand this. He asked Americans to follow CDC guidelines (which at the time discouraged the wearing of masks) but respected the right of each American to personalize the application of those guidelines according to his own needs.

This mixture between federalism and general compliance was a good approach to the problem. But it just wasn't enough for some of the nation's mayors and governors. Gaining compliance is easier and faster with force instead of persuasion, and many took the position that the end (ensuring public health) justified the means (disregarding religious rights). The precedent set by abrogating rights guaranteed by the Constitution was an afterthought.

Never was this more apparent than in an April 15, 2020, exchange between Fox News prime-time opinion host Tucker Carlson and Democratic New Jersey governor Phil Murphy. Carlson, referring to the arrest of fifteen congregants at a synagogue in New Jersey, inquired of Governor Murphy, saying, "By what authority did you nullify the Bill of Rights in issuing this order? How do you have the power to do that?"

The governor responded, "That's above my pay grade, Tucker. I wasn't thinking of the Bill of Rights when we did this."

Carlson asked again. "How do you have the authority to order something that so clearly contravenes the Bill of Rights of the United States, the U.S. Constitution? Where do you get the authority to do that?"

Governor Murphy replied with a series of persuasive justifications—that they knew people needed to stay away from each other, that they had broad authority to enforce that provision, and that they coordinated with a diverse group of faith leaders about the policy.

Carlson wasn't satisfied, responding,

> I'm just going to ask you one last time because I think it's important. I'm sure you've thought about this. You can't just, as the governor of a state, tell people who they can talk to when and where because the Constitution of the United States, upon which all of this is based, prohibits you from doing that. So you clearly decided that you could do it. Did you consult an attorney about this? Because this is a legal question as well as a medical one.

Though Murphy assured him he doesn't go to the men's room without consulting an attorney, he could only offer ends-justify-the-means arguments for why he was able to abridge the rights of his citizens to peaceably assemble for worship.

The truth is, though the justifications are true and real, Attorney General William Barr was correct when he told us "the Constitution is not suspended in times of crisis." Governments are not allowed to single out worship services for restrictions. But they did.

The right to religious exercise underwent one of its greatest tests as the case for states to forcibly compel shutdowns of church services became a matter of life and death. The harder government pushed the use of force, the more Americans were galvanized to push back and defend their rights.

Two core rights—freedom of religion and freedom to assemble—were pitted against Christlike virtues of charity and love. After all, how can someone claim to be charitable and simultaneously risk spreading a deadly virus?

The question was not so black-and-white for some parishioners, who believed the risk could be mitigated with social distancing, hand washing, masks, or outdoor services. For these people, church services were more than just a chance to study the word of God. They were a source of strength, emotional support, connection, and love. They offered justifications of their own— that there were few cases of the disease in their area, that they were low risk, or that they were willing to risk life for liberty.

All across America the conflict between public health and religious worship intensified. With the initial spread of the virus in South Korea being traced to a worship service, legitimate questions arose about a very subjective question. Is church attendance necessary to human life? If Wal-Mart is open and essential for physical sustenance, who gets to decide whether and under what conditions church should be open for spiritual sustenance?

The Courts Chasten State Overreach

The answer to these questions, of course, is yes, religion is essential—and public worship is a vital part of religious practice. To infringe upon a right to gather in a way that singles out people of faith is to violate the rights that the Constitution outlines. The courts made this clear in 2020.

Let me explain this distinction in the law. The First

Amendment protects the "free exercise" of religion. Governors cannot regulate religious beliefs or punish religious activity with the purpose of disapproving a specific religion or religion in general. But the courts *have* held that they can regulate religious actions using laws that apply broadly to all and not specifically to those practicing their faith. In *Employment Division v. Smith*, the Supreme Court held that two members of a Native American faith who used peyote as a sacrament could be denied unemployment benefits under a broad law prohibiting the use of drugs by beneficiaries. Under that standard, general emergency orders prohibiting in-person gatherings broadly, which are neutral with respect to religion, can be constitutional.

That wasn't good enough for many governors and mayors. In New York, Governor Andrew Cuomo crossed the line. He started with a broad order, which was fine. On March 23, 2020, he limited socially distanced outdoor religious services in a broadly worded order that banned "nonessential gatherings of individuals of any size for any reason," which included religious gatherings. That wasn't what got him in trouble with the courts.

In the process of slowly reopening, Cuomo made the mistake of singling out religious activity. In May, he permitted religious gatherings of up to ten people if socially distanced as well as drive-in services outside, provided no one left their cars. When he allowed business on his "phase II" list to reopen at 50 percent capacity, the list excluded religious gatherings. Within days of that order, Black Lives Matter protests erupted, with support from both Cuomo and New York City mayor Bill de Blasio. A week later, on June 6, Cuomo added religious gatherings to his order for phase II reopenings, but only at 25 percent capacity. That meant activities like haircuts and shopping were subject to fewer restrictions than constitutionally protected religious exercise. It also meant First Amendment speech protections were being used to justify protests, but not religious exercise.

The courts rightly intervened. In late June, U.S. district court judge Gary Sharpe issued an injunction blocking enforcement of Cuomo's order. Sharpe's injunction prohibited restrictions on outdoor gatherings and ordered the state not to subject indoor religious gatherings to greater restrictions than other phase II activities. In his ruling, he cited comments Cuomo made at a June 1 press conference telling protesters, "You can do many things now as long as you're smart about it, right?" The judge further implicated Cuomo's statement to New Yorkers to "be smart. It does not mean you go to a temple or a mosque and you sit right next to a person. You have to socially distance." Sharpe also cited comments from Mayor de Blasio on April 28, in which he tweeted against those gathered for a funeral in the Williamsburg section of Brooklyn, writing, "What I saw WILL NOT be tolerated so long as we are fighting Coronavirus." De Blasio singled out the Orthodox funeral even as hundreds of Williamsburg hipsters had gathered in the trendy neighborhood's Domino Park on April 20. He added, "My message to the Jewish community, and all communities, is this simple: the time for warnings has passed. I have instructed NYPD to proceed immediately to summons or even arrest those who gather in large groups. This is about stopping this disease and saving lives. Period." Then, weeks later, a maskless de Blasio addressed a gathering of Black Lives Matter protesters.

"By acting as they did, Governor Cuomo and Mayor de Blasio sent a clear message that mass protests are deserving of preferential treatment," wrote Judge Sharpe. The lawyer for the plaintiffs, which had included Catholic clergy as well as Orthodox Jewish congregants, described Cuomo's order as a "sham" that "went right out the window as soon as he and Mayor de Blasio saw a mass protest movement they favored taking to the streets by the thousands." The attorney, Christopher Ferrara, went on to highlight the hypocrisy of the discriminatory orders against religious exercise.

Suddenly, the limit on "mass gatherings" was no longer necessary to "save lives." Yet they were continuing to ban high
school graduations and other outdoor gatherings exceeding a
mere 25 people. This decision is an important step toward
inhibiting the suddenly emerging trend of exercising absolute
monarchy on pretext of public health. What this kind of regime
really meant in practice is freedom for me, but not for thee.

Similar lawsuits proliferated around the nation. In Oregon, ten
churches filed suit against Governor Kate Brown's "Stay-Home-
Save-Lives" emergency orders, alleging "irreparable harm" from
the prohibition against religious exercise. Baker County judge
Matthew B. Shirtcliff ruled the governor's orders exceeded a
twenty-eight-day limit imposed by state lawmakers, and that the
orders were no longer valid. In response to an appeal from the
governor's office, the state Supreme Court stayed Shirtcliff's ruling, ensuring the restrictions would remain in place until the high
court could consider the petition. Shirtcliff found that churches
were just as capable of taking precautions against disease spread
as other essential businesses.

A similar lawsuit against California governor Gavin Newsom accused the governor of "criminalizing church attendance"
with broad stay-at-home orders while granting "sweeping exceptions" for favored businesses and professions.

"If a Californian is able to go to Costco or the local marijuana shop or liquor store and buy goods in a responsible, socially
distanced manner, then he or she must be allowed to practice
their faith using the same precautions," said chief executive of
the Center for American Liberty Harmeet K. Dhillon, who filed
the lawsuit on behalf of California parishioners and plaintiffs,
one of whom was fined $1,000 for holding a Palm Sunday service
in Riverside County. This time federal judge Cynthia A. Bashant
ruled that freedom of religion does not protect the right to expose the community to communicable diseases.

Yet another lawsuit against Newsom challenged a July 1, 2020, ban on singing and chanting in places of religious worship. As of this writing, that lawsuit is one of many challenging coronavirus restrictions that await resolution.

Give an Inch, the Government Will Take a Mile

As is often the case in a free society, there were extremes in both the failure to uphold rights and the failure to uphold responsibilities. As defenders of civil liberties so often warn, government couldn't seem to resist overstepping authority. As statists love to point out, advocates of liberty in some cases used their freedom to put others at risk.

But on the government side, once government officials felt empowered to suspend rights for our own good, they kept taking more. Not content to simply prohibit public church services, politicians (many of them Democrats) immediately began embracing draconian measures to enforce the quarantine.

In Kentucky, Democrat governor Andy Beshear warned he would authorize state officials to force residents into a fourteen-day quarantine if they attended Easter services, going so far as to announce that government would record license plates of churchgoers and turn them over to the health department. The threat rekindled memories of China welding people into their apartments in Wuhan, willing to let them die there rather than risk spreading the contagion. The image is a visceral reminder of what a powerful government can do when rights are no longer protected. The following week, a federal judge issued a temporary restraining order against Louisville mayor Greg Fischer for his efforts to ban drive-in Easter services. U.S. district court judge Justin Walker called the policy "stunning" and "beyond all reason unconstitutional."

In Greenville, Mississippi, where the King James Bible Baptist Church held a Thursday evening drive-in church service, police reportedly surrounded the church parking lot to enforce Mayor Errick Simmons's curfew law. Parishioners stayed in their cars with windows rolled up listening to the broadcast on a local radio frequency but were still harassed by police. At nearby Temple Baptist Church, police issued $500 tickets—one to each individual in each vehicle. A husband and wife sitting together in a car faced a $1,000 fine. In the face of intense public backlash, Mayor Simmons later rescinded the fines, bristling at allegations that his intent was to target churches.

Even as late as July, churches came under fire in California with an order from Democratic governor Gavin Newsom that banned singing and chanting at religious worship services. A week later, he expanded the order to ban worship altogether, even in private homes, for those living in counties that encompass 80 percent of the state's population. Even visiting a fellow parishioner to study the Bible in their home became a crime. Violations of those orders came with $1,000 fines, criminal charges, and up to a year in jail. Some pastors in that state face thousands of dollars in fines for exercising rights guaranteed by the Constitution.

While government leaders were failing to uphold the rights of liberty, a small minority of Americans were failing to uphold the responsibilities of liberty. Most who protested in favor of their right to religious exercise did so responsibly—following CDC guidelines to protect those around them. But a few openly defied social distancing guidelines and packed large worship services. In Florida, Rev. Rodney Howard-Browne was arrested after hundreds gathered at his Pentecostal megachurch, packed shoulder to shoulder, according to the *Tampa Bay Times*. Police cited Howard-Browne's "reckless disregard for human life." Republican sheriff Chad Chronister said, "Our goal here is not to stop anyone from worshiping, but the safety and well-being of our community must always come first."

Was it wrong for government to crack down on worshipers? Was it wrong for devout Americans to gather together for support in a time of national distress? In America, we each decide for ourselves. We try the questions in the court of public opinion and in the court systems of the United States of America. Everyone gets to have and express an opinion. When one side or the other goes too far, public backlash can have a more powerful and immediate effect than the use of force. Legal remedies can also settle the question.

In the case of Governor J. B. Pritzker's coronavirus response in Illinois, one church fought back, challenging the governor's stay-at-home order in court. In response, Governor Pritzker revised the stay-at-home order, classifying worship services as essential under certain conditions. "When we started the day, Illinois was one of 10 states that entirely banned religious services," said Peter Breen, vice president and senior counsel for the Thomas More Society, which funded the lawsuit. "We couldn't even drive on a church parking lot. In fact, you couldn't even leave your house to go to a church service. Now you can do that. And, in fact, the executive order now encourages people to have drive-in services; which is a great recommendation, I'm glad that they added it."

Suspending the Constitution

In the face of a deadly virus, some felt they were being forced to choose between life and liberty. It's not a question of, "Give me liberty or give me death," as Patrick Henry famously said. For many people, choosing liberty could literally be choosing death.

On the other hand, the Constitution offers no exceptions for times of crisis. The question is not whether this particular crisis offers good enough reasons to suspend our rights. The question is whether we want to set the precedent that government has the authority to revoke those rights.

President Kennedy affirmed in his inaugural address that "the rights of man come not from the generosity of the state but from the hand of God." If we allow the state to subjectively dictate when those rights can be recognized, we open ourselves up to political manipulation and abuse. We create an opening through which tyranny can enter. The question of when rights can be suspended is a subjective one as well as a political one. Given the animosity between the left and right in this country, is there any question some of the most powerful would use the opportunity to suspend basic rights for political gain?

The real danger of using force to prohibit worship services is the damage done to the constitutional order. The price of that damage may seem small today in comparison to the human lives at stake. But eventually, the virus will be quelled. The constitutional implications of suspending individual rights could have far-reaching consequences. In some ways, this debate was a choice between immediate negative consequences and long-term catastrophic ones.

Respecting Religious Freedom

During my life, I have had periods when I have been spiritually dormant, and times I have been spiritually devout. Today I pray, but you might not. I go to church, but you might not. I pay a tithing to my church, but you might not. I have been on both sides of those equations.

I grew up in a religiously agnostic home. During my young life I did have religious experiences, but it took until later in life to understand and recognize them as religious in nature. I didn't fully embrace my religious beliefs and reliance on God until I was in my twenties. Today I do faithfully practice my Christian beliefs, and I do so because I choose to.

Along the way, I have found this to be very helpful in being empathetic to those who choose to practice differently than I do, or who elect not to practice at all. That's part of the miracle of the United States of America. Government does not thrust religion upon us, nor does it deny us our beliefs. We have freedom to make a choice, and this is a cornerstone of our foundation and our Bill of Rights.

I respect those who chose to stay at home during the lockdown. I also respect those who believed they needed their religious community during dark days. Our form of government requires us to go to the work of threading the needle to balance rights and responsibilities without the use of force.

Where do we go from here? The answer is not for one side to win and the other side to lose. America has never worked that way. In a battle over two competing values, each side of this debate will fight to prioritize one or the other. Each will check the excesses of the other. But ultimately, the courts will decide the degree to which our First Amendment rights are preserved and protected. Religious liberty is just the first of those rights. It wasn't the only one the pandemic would challenge. Nor was it the only one that offered a political opportunity to create new precedents in restricting liberty.

CHAPTER II

CHILLING FREE SPEECH

Among the more alarming impacts of disaster liberalism is the punitive response to unpopular speech. The desire to punish or retaliate against those who hold opposing views gains traction in a time of crisis. Gaining public support for penalizing those who reject a prevailing narrative is easier when the matter can be described as life-or-death. And that's exactly what 2020 provided. Power-mad politicians didn't just target religious gatherings, but more generally those whose speech didn't fit.

In an age of cancel culture and polarized politics, we encounter countless stories of people who suspect they have been retaliated against for their political beliefs. But Dimple and Denis Navratil of Racine, Wisconsin, don't have to suspect. They have it in writing.

The owners of a downtown Racine import business, the Navratils were twice denied municipal emergency assistance funding designed to help local businesses. The first time they were told there just wasn't enough money for all the businesses that applied. Which was true-ish. But after the second denial, they learned they were deliberately excluded from consideration, despite meeting all required criteria, because they attended a rally to speak out against Governor Tony Evers's doomed Safer at Home order.

The city couched it as a "compliance" issue. The governor's order, which forcibly closed businesses like the Navratils while allowing their larger competitors to remain open, restricted "nonessential" travel. The couple had traveled two hours to Madison for a protest. The governor's extended order would later be struck down and invalidated by the Wisconsin Supreme Court. But by then it would be too late for the Navratils.

Racine mayor Cory Mason, a Democrat, actually put the admission in writing. In a statement, the man who would later respond with alacrity to the demands of Black Lives Matter protesters violating restrictions in his own town wrote of the Navratils:

> Participating in mass gatherings outside of our community, such as the rally that was held at the State Capitol—such large gatherings have been linked to cases of COVID-19 around the state—and then returning to our City, only served to put our residents at unnecessary risk and, thus, factored into the funding consideration.

The local newspaper, the *Journal Times*, filed an open records request that revealed no scoring system had been used in awarding grant recipients and no notes or minutes of the decision-making process were kept. The city had distributed some $900,000 to more than 150 local businesses, ranging from $2,500 to $15,000 each.

After admitting the city had retaliated against the couple as a result of their exercise of free speech, the mayor went on to assure the Navratils he was still an advocate of free speech.

> While I certainly support the rights of free speech and assembly, I cannot in good conscience send scarce City resources to

a person or business that willingly jeopardized public health, especially when they were competing with other businesses who were not flagrantly violating safety measures.

As for the protesters, some of whom would later flagrantly burn down the Community-Oriented Policing House in Racine, Mayor Mason could not act fast enough to respond to their demands. After protesters gathered together right there in Racine to throw rocks and launch fireworks at police, Mason quickly pledged "immediate action on police reform." As for those scarce city resources that Mason needed to so carefully protect, he pledged $47,500 out of the police budget to pay a consulting firm who would facilitate a task force. The task force would respond to the demands of the many protesters who, by the standard applied to Navratils, "willingly jeopardized public health."

It wasn't just the retaliation against the Navratils that was chilling, but the complete selectivity in how various protests were treated. This is not an isolated incident. Time and again, we see self-proclaimed defenders of free speech deploy strategies to enable the suppression of speech they don't like. Two strategies that were prominent in 2020 were the selective application of rules and the labeling of mainstream ideas as extreme or dangerous.

Freedom of Speech . . . for Some

American philosopher Noam Chomsky famously said, "If we do not believe in freedom of speech for those we despise we do not believe in it at all."

The Black Lives Matter protests exposed just how many of our elected officials defend the concept of free speech, but don't believe in free speech at all when it comes to opposing views. They want plaudits for upholding the free speech rights of rioters,

vandals, and looters among the peaceful protesters, but they re-
act very differently toward protesters whose causes they don't
support. The examples are too numerous to catalog exhaustively,
but we can highlight a few.

California governor Gavin Newsom had a very different reaction to lockdown protesters than he did to Black Lives Matter
groups. His stay-at-home order was issued on March 19, 2020,
prohibiting large gatherings. One month later, with the economy
in rapid decline and no end in sight to the lockdown, protesters
received a permit to gather at the State Capitol Building in Sacramento. Hundreds reportedly drove vehicles around the capitol complex, honking horns and holding up signs. Some stood
"shoulder-to-shoulder" cheering them on.

In response, the California Highway Patrol announced in a
statement they would no longer issue permits for protests because
"the permit for the convoy was issued with the understanding
that the protest would be conducted in a manner consistent with
the state's public health guidance. That is not what occurred."

At a news conference the following Monday, Newsom laid
down strict expectations for protests in the state. "If you're going
to protest," he said, "practice physical distancing. If you're going
to protest and express your right of free speech, do so in a way
that protects your health and the health of others." The *Sacramento Bee* helpfully reminded readers that public health experts
say protests against the stay-at-home directive could harm the
state's battle against the virus. In response to calls to reopen the
economy, Newsom said prophetically, "We must have a health-
first focus if we're ultimately going to come back economically.
The worst mistake we can make is making a precipitous decision
based on politics and frustration that puts people's lives at risk
and ultimately sets back the cause of economic growth and economic recovery."

Of course, all of that went out the window as soon as new

protests began that aligned with Newsom's political interests. Though Newsom would be among the last to reopen his state's economy, he would promote the gathering of thousands in violation of his own orders. After the first weekend of violent riots, Newsom condemned the violence, but told BLM protesters, "Your rage is real. Express it so that we can hear it." That was a far cry from the message he sent to lockdown protesters.

He made the "precipitous decision based on politics" to treat racial protests differently from others. As he predicted, it "ultimately set back the cause of economic growth and recovery" as California experienced a surge in new cases in the weeks following the Black Lives Matter protests. Both Los Angeles mayor Eric Garcetti and county public health director Dr. Barbara Ferrer acknowledged a connection between the protests and the subsequent surge in new cases weeks later.

In response to the lockdown protest at the state capitol in April, California state senator Richard Pan, a pediatrician and a Democrat, explained why protests were so dangerous. "We know this disease, when people cluster together for periods of time, is how it spreads," he said. "That's why we have the orders not to gather. There's a certain level of selfishness and lack of concern for other people and that's concerning."

As soon as I read that quotation, reported in the *Sacramento Bee*, I questioned whether Pan had responded similarly to the protests that began a month later—the ones that supported his political narrative. Who are we kidding? I didn't need to wonder. We all know what I would find. Sure enough, there was a tweet.

Pan posted a photo on June 6 of himself standing shoulder to shoulder with dozens of others holding a professionally printed sign that read, "Health Care Workers for Black Lives." Granted, they all posed carefully in their masks. But by then, the state had been denying permits to other protesters for a month without offering any exceptions for those who commit to wear masks.

Ron Givens and Christine Bish were among those denied permits to protest due to Newsom's stay-at-home order, which initially banned all gatherings. Newsom's order was later revised to allow groups of one hundred people or 2 percent of a venue's maximum capacity—whichever was less. Givens, a firearms instructor, hoped to protest delays in processing background checks for gun purchasers. Bish, a 2020 congressional candidate, sought a protest to call for pandemic restrictions to be lifted. The requests to stage peaceful protests were denied.

In late April, long before the Black Lives Matter protests would expose the lockdown double standard for all to see, the Center for American Liberty would sue Newsom for denying Givens and Bish their First and Fourteenth Amendment rights. The lawsuit claimed Newsom's lockdown orders were not being enforced in a viewpoint-neutral manner. In June, the Department of Justice (DOJ) filed a friend-of-the-court brief in the case seeking to invalidate Newsom's order. DOJ argued California had allowed protests in violation of state orders and should not hold other protests to a different standard. One DOJ official told Fox News, "The First Amendment does not allow California to selectively enforce its protest rules by allowing large gatherings of over 100—often without permits—in response to the Floyd tragedy, and at the same time, apply tougher rules to other protests, such as those by Givens and Bish."

In a May 19 *New York Times* op-ed, constitutional lawyers Floyd Abrams and John Langford warned of the potential against unconstitutional lockdown orders, specifically pointing to California. As of May 8, they said, the state had permitted the reopening of bookstores, clothing stores, and more while continuing to restrict gatherings and protests. Their advice to states like California (just ten days before racial protests would erupt across the nation) was to narrowly tailor restrictions. The state could have permitted protests on the condition that individuals abide by social distancing guidelines and mask rules. They could have reasonably limited the number of protesters so that social distancing would be feasible.

Instead, Newsom in July 2020 banned singing and chanting at places of worship. The order is quite specific. "Places of worship must therefore discontinue singing and chanting activities," it read.

Would any of us have believed at the beginning of 2020 that we would see a state governor order people to stop singing at church? Would we have thought we lived in a country where such a restriction was even legal?

And who would enforce such an order? The demoralized police forces whom California officials have accused of overreach? Once again, the attempt to use the force of government to prohibit constitutionally protected activities is bad enough. But when that abuse of power is directed selectively at some populations and not others, that is the very recipe for tyranny.

Similar stories were playing out in other jurisdictions around the country. In New Jersey, Kim Pagan was arrested in April for organizing a small protest in which cars honked horns, people chanted while holding signs, and (gasp) two men were said to have embraced! That was April. By early June, Governor Phil Murphy himself was marching side by side with protesters in violation of his own order. While he had routinely referred to violators of his orders as "knuckleheads" in his daily briefings, Murphy had nothing but praise for the protesters whose politics aligned with his. "We have to recognize this moment in time," he said, justifying the mass gatherings throughout the state. "This is unlike any moment in our history. We have to acknowledge that. We have to allow folks to get out there rightfully and peacefully," he said.

Orwellian Language

But seeking to silence opposing voices wasn't the only strategy for suppressing wrongthink in the wake of the public health crisis. There's another strategy that takes mainstream political ideas—ideas that have been the norm throughout American history—and repackages them as something dangerous, extreme, and unutterable in polite society. At the same time, radical leftist riots are euphemized as peaceful protests. War is peace. Ignorance is strength. Freedom is slavery.

This is not a new strategy. For years, those who believe there should be rules and boundaries governing immigration into this country, or penalties for immigrants who commit crimes, have been labeled xenophobic. Those who believe the nuclear family is the building block of society—a view that has been mainstream in America, and indeed throughout human history—were labeled homophobic. Those who question whether biological males should be able to compete against biological females in sporting competitions were labeled transphobes. Those who support policies to vet immigrants coming from countries with a history of terrorist activity were called Islamophobes. Those who do not support broad schemes to redistribute wealth, who support enforcement of the rule of law, or who oppose the legalization of drugs and prostitution were labeled racists. These are all mainstream views that have been labeled dangerous, socially unacceptable, and worthy of suppression.

Meanwhile, this strategy also works in reverse. During the months of anti-police protesting, many of us came to understand that if the media had to tell us the protest was peaceful, it probably wasn't. Headlines like this one from ABC News in late July were typical. "Protesters in California Set Fire to a Courthouse, Damaged a Police Station and Assaulted Officers After a Peaceful

Demonstration Intensified." To which the *Wall Street Journal*'s James Taranto sardonically replied in a tweet, "It became even more intensely peaceful."

By contrast, earlier demonstrations in Michigan protesting Governor Gretchen Whitmer's restrictive lockdown orders were characterized in the most violent terms. Headlines breathlessly proclaimed "armed protesters" had entered the capitol building during an April 30 protest, implying the protests had been violent. They weren't.

Typical of the characterization of those protests was that of Washington representative Pramila Jayapal during her July 2020 questioning of Attorney General Bill Barr. Jayapal was upset with Barr for the presence of federal law enforcement at anti-police protests in Portland. There, protesters brandishing powerful lasers had blinded police, repeatedly set fire to the federal building while people were inside, and deployed Tasers, pellet guns, and slingshots according to Barr. But Jayapal wanted to know why Barr had not deployed federal law enforcement to the May 1 anti-lockdown protests in Michigan. She described them this way:

> [I]n Michigan, when protesters carried guns and Confederate flags and swastikas and call for the governor of Michigan to be beheaded and shot and lynched, somehow, you're not aware of that. Somehow, you didn't know about that, so you didn't send federal agents in to do to the president's supporters what you did to the president's protesters.

That sounds like a wild protest. But it wasn't. No one was arrested. No fires were set. No police or protesters were injured at any of the lockdown protests in Michigan. No gunshots were heard. There was a small scuffle during one of the protests, which was efficiently dispatched by Michigan State Police without injuries.

As for the swastika, that was the most misleading claim of all. It was so humiliatingly debunked, it's shocking that Jayapal dared use it. Even leftist fact-checker Snopes.com had to acknowledge the swastika claim was fake news. "This appears to be a genuine photograph," read the fact check. "However, it was not taken in Lansing, Michigan, during Operation Gridlock in April 2020 and it may not actually show a Trump supporter."

Snopes.com later updated the fact check with this information about the man holding the swastika sign: "Additional images from the event appear to show that this person was holding a Bernie Sanders sign at another point during the rally."

Yet the left attempted to define the entire rally by that one person holding a single sign—a sign that wasn't actually there. Meanwhile, organized bands of violent rioters can take over blue cities night after night, distributing weapons and injuring people, and they are characterized as a separate entity from the "mostly peaceful protesters."

Contrast the lack of violence in Michigan with the realities of Portland, where even the *New York Times* admits that by July 22, twenty-eight federal officers had been injured. Or Seattle, where protesters took over a police precinct. In July police recovered improvised explosive devices (IEDs) in a van from which protesters had been distributing supplies. Among the items being supplied were bear and pepper spray, pyrotechnics, stun guns, and improvised spike strips. Some sixty officers were injured in late July riots during which a bomb was thrown into the East Precinct building.

Despite depictions of peaceful protesters, both cities were a war zone for months. Citing a court filing from the U.S. attorney's office in Oregon, the *New York Times* reported one federal officer in Portland was struck in the head by a protester wielding a two-pound sledgehammer. The protester had been attempting to break down a door to the Hatfield Courthouse. The filing indicated other injuries, including "broken bones, hearing damage, eye damage, a dislocated shoulder, sprains, strains, and contusions." In his July testimony, Attorney General Barr described one U.S. marshal who was hit with a pellet gun that penetrated "to the bone."

But that's not what news reports were suggesting. The *New York Times* painted the Portland protests as mostly peaceful until federal law enforcement arrived, thus making the Trump administration responsible for the violence. "Peaceful protests were already happening for weeks when federal officers arrived on July 4," the *Times* explained, failing to mention the violence, police assaults, and consistent attacks on the federal building that drew federal enforcement in the first place.

The propaganda of mostly peaceful protests became so pervasive that Republican lawmakers feared many Americans might actually believe it. Not everyone was shocked when Democrat House Judiciary Committee chairman Jerry Nadler of New York told writer-producer Austin Fletcher on camera that Antifa rioting and violence in Portland was a myth. That was the narrative. But I imagine more than a few were shocked when the committee's ranking member Jim Jordan used his opening statement in the July hearing with Attorney General Barr to show video footage of the brutality. The video included clips Republicans felt leftist media outlets had suppressed. The narrative of mostly peaceful protests, despite its obvious conflict with the truth, had been widely reported.

It wasn't just Portland, either. Leftist protests in general were frequently described as "mostly peaceful." Commentator Ben Shapiro highlighted this head scratcher from the *Los Angeles Times* following the riots that ensued from George Floyd's murder. The *Times* wrote, "The third night of countywide curfews followed days of massive, mostly peaceful protests. . . . Nearly 1,200 people were arrested Sunday after police officers clashed with demonstrators and looters shattered windows and emptied stores in Santa Monica and Long Beach." Shapiro explained, "In truth, the category of 'mostly peaceful' is a brand-new invention meant to obscure the simple fact that many of our cultural elites are fine with violence so long as those who engage in such violence have the proper goals."

There's that double standard again. One headline in the *Babylon Bee* captured the absurdity of the reporting. "Orcs March on Minas Tirith in Mostly Peaceful Protest," it heralded, referencing the epic final battle scene in the *Lord of the Rings* saga.

The rhetoric used to describe the various riots flies in the face of the facts. But it's one more way to suppress speech without actually having to take on the First Amendment directly. It's a strategy that only works if the media is on board.

And they are.

The video shown to the world by Republicans during the congressional hearing with Attorney General Barr in July featured an extensive super-cut of various news organizations using the term "mostly peaceful protests," overlaid with actual video of the violence perpetrated by rioters. The media's seemingly coordinated messaging promotes the pernicious notion that violent protests are actually peaceful, mainstream, and justified. Meanwhile, right-wing political views are characterized as extreme, dangerous, and worthy of being ruthlessly rooted out. Hence the labeling of popular political views as racist, bigoted, or my favorite—on the wrong side of history. Such characterizations make it easy to rationalize the suppression of mainstream views that stand in the way of leftist policies, interest groups, and donors.

Suppressing Views Is Bad for Everyone

So what is lost in this ideological suppression? Like the Marxist ideology so many protesters embrace that leaves empty store shelves and limited choices, the war on opposing ideas leaves America bereft. There is danger in suppressing the views of large swaths of the American electorate. And not just because it could lead to the election of someone like Donald J. Trump—though that argument is legitimately persuasive to leftists. Nate Silver at FiveThirtyEight argued that lack of diversity and independence among political journalists contributed to groupthink that underestimated Trump's appeal in 2016.

But the other danger is that suppressing unpopular ideas gives the suppressors a feeling of uncontested power and self-righteousness. You don't have to look hard to understand that liberalism in America has become illiberal. What was once a political and moral philosophy that valued liberty is now used as a label for those who would do the opposite. Liberals today argue for suppressing and even penalizing speech they find offensive, religious practices they find abhorrent, and gatherings with which they disagree. College campuses, once a bastion of traditional liberalism, have become ground zero in the effort to suppress ideas. The notion of liberalism is now inextricably linked with a punitive response to opposing ideas.

This illiberalism was fostered in America's universities. George Washington University professor Jonathan Turley, in testimony before the Senate Judiciary Committee's Subcommittee on the Constitution, testified about the impact of 2020 protests at college campuses.

In my three decades of teaching, I have never seen the level of fear and intimidation that we have today on our campuses.

Many professors are afraid to voice dissenting views of the
current protests or other issues out of fear that they could be
accused of racism or even physically attacked. Some professors have indeed been assaulted or required police protection
after voicing opposing views. To put it simply, Antifa and these
other extremist groups are winning, and few people seem to
be taking notice.

In his classic book, *On Liberty*, philosopher John Stuart
Mill worried that truth not debated or challenged would become
"dead dogma." He argued that when we refuse to engage dissenting viewpoints, the "living power" of our own opinions is lost.
Without other available perspectives to challenge us, we aren't
able to think critically about why we believe what we do. So
it is ironic that those who call themselves liberals have become
primary proponents of what has come to be known as "cancel
culture."

Retaliation and Cancellation

What's wrong with our young people? *Business leaders who donate to Donald Trump or Joe Biden should be fired.* At least, that
is the view of a surprisingly high number of people under the age
of thirty who responded to a July poll from YouGov and the
Cato Institute. Forty-four percent of adults under thirty in the
poll said donating to Trump should be a firing offense. Voting
for Biden would be a firing offense to 27 percent of respondents
in that age bracket. Among strong liberals of all age brackets,
50 percent support firing executives who personally donate to
Trump. Cato director of polling Emily Elkins reported that more
than 50 percent of poll respondents of both parties indicated they

had opinions they were afraid to share—52 percent of Democrats and 59 percent of Republicans.

Why? Because such retaliation has become a political tool. Not just in political careers, but in media, popular culture, and academia. In the confusing days following the November presidential election, when ballots continued to be counted and outcomes disputed, a surprising number of leftist thought leaders actually verbalized a desire to retaliate against anyone who openly supported President Trump. New York Democratic representative Alexandria Ocasio-Cortez tweeted three days after the election, "Is anyone archiving these Trump sycophants for when they try to downplay or deny their complicity in the future? I foresee decent probability of many deleted Tweets, writings, photos in the future."

Someone had already beaten her to it. A reply to her tweet from Michael Simon read,

> Yes, we are.
>   The Trump Accountability Project (@trumpaccproject)
>   Every Administration staffer, campaign staffer, bundler, lawyer who represented them—everyone. https://t.co/PHx8 v8GxOp

Indeed, the link initially took readers to a spreadsheet listing names and categories of people who supported Trump, including federal judges. In another message that day, Emily Abrams wrote, "We're launching the Trump Accountability Project to make sure anyone who took a paycheck to help Trump undermine America is held responsible for what they did. Join us and help spread the word."

The bandwagon got bigger, with *Washington Post* columnist and renowned Trump Derangement Syndrome sufferer Jennifer Rubin chiming in,

Any R now promoting rejection of an election or calling to
not to follow the will of voters or making baseless allegations
of fraud should never serve in office, join a corporate board,
find a faculty position or be accepted into "polite" society. We
have a list.

Coming as they did just ahead of an invitation by self-
proclaimed president-elect Joe Biden to heal and unite, these
messages let Americans know that free speech was not for everyone. As George Orwell explained in *Animal Farm*, "All animals
are equal. But some animals are more equal than others."

The *New York Times* masquerades as an essential organ
of free speech in this country, but as it turns out, the gray lady
can't tolerate even the most cordial of dissenters. Former *New
York Times* opinion editor Bari Weiss articulated the challenges
faced in her profession by those who don't toe the line on leftist narratives. Weiss was hired after 2016 produced a spate of
self-reflection among the *Times*' management. Long regarded as
the "paper of record" in this country, the *Times* got 2016 all
wrong. In a letter of apology to its readers, publisher Arthur
Sulzberger Jr. acknowledged his paper's failure to prepare readers for the possibility of a Trump victory. "After such an erratic
and unpredictable election," he wrote, "there are inevitable questions: Did Donald Trump's sheer unconventionality lead us and
other news outlets to underestimate his support among American
voters?" Sulzberger pledged to readers that the paper would "aim
to rededicate" itself to the fundamental mission of journalism, to
"report America and the world honestly, without fear or favor,
striving always to understand and reflect all political perspectives." To that end, the paper hired Weiss in 2017 to represent
"voices that would not otherwise appear" in the paper's pages.

But staffers at the *New York Times* apparently couldn't tolerate the centrist views of Bari Weiss. Weiss said she endured

"constant bullying" from colleagues, and that her work was "openly demeaned," she was called a Nazi and a racist, and subjected to anti-Semitic comments. Her crime? Wrongthink.

John Podhoretz, in a column for the *New York Post*, described Weiss's political views. "Weiss, who is a friend of mine, is not a conservative," he writes. "She calls herself a centrist, and as someone who has argued with her on matters of ideology, I can confirm this is an entirely fair description. She is, however, versed in conservative thinking and argument and open to both. This is a thought-crime in woke circles."

In her letter to Sulzberger, resigning her position at the *Times* in July 2020, Weiss called the newspaper out for failing to learn the lessons of 2016.

> But the lessons that ought to have followed the election—lessons about the importance of understanding other Americans, the necessity of resisting tribalism, and the centrality of the free exchange of ideas to a democratic society—have not been learned. Instead, a new consensus has emerged in the press, but perhaps especially at this paper: that truth isn't a process of collective discovery, but an orthodoxy already known to an enlightened few whose job is to inform everyone else.

Of the Paper of Record, Weiss says, "Showing up for work as a centrist at an American newspaper should not require bravery."

Others within the organization have also acknowledged the problem. *New York Times* columnist Nicholas Kristof in 2016 wrote a column acknowledging that leftist calls for diversity excluded diversity of thought. "We're fine with people who don't look like us," he wrote, "as long as they think like us."

He described a recent Facebook post in which he had questioned whether stigmatizing conservatives at universities undermined intellectual diversity. The responses he got were scathing. "Truth has a liberal slant," one person had written.

Kristof was troubled by the response. "When perspectives are unrepresented in discussions, when some kinds of thinkers aren't at the table, classrooms become echo chambers rather than sounding boards—and we all lose," he wrote.

The comments to his column from *New York Times* readers bore out those concerns. Arnie in Burlington, Vermont, wrote, "I am sorry, but conservative values and belief systems are the antithesis of what academia is all about." A woman in Oregon suggested conservatives "are not rationally intellectually engaged." Another reader said conservatives are anti-education and anti-science. "We need fewer in academia, not more," he wrote. A New Jersey reader added, "Reality does in fact have a liberal bias." Eric in Detroit suggested it wasn't intolerant to "insist that candidates for a job should be competent. And increasingly, support of Republican policies and worldview is incompatible with competence in a broad variety of fields." Someone posting as WestSider in NYC noted, "I associate 'conservative' with close mindedness, bigotry and religious fanaticism." He was one of many readers who believed religious conviction disqualified people from academic engagement. "No scientist holds groundless beliefs to prove some kind of subservience to a deity," wrote one reader.

Which brings us to the ivory tower. These attitudes influence what gets produced in academia. Even if conservatives manage to get hired, some report being intimidated and silenced.

In the wake of the Black Lives Matter protests, one black history professor publicly posted an anonymous letter to the department heads at the University of California, Berkeley, contesting their one-sided narrative regarding the protests. Given the overwhelming dominance of progressive orthodoxy in academia, the professor opened by explaining why the letter was anonymous.

"I am worried that writing this email publicly might lead to me losing my job, and likely all future jobs in my field."

If there is any place in America where the marketplace of ideas should be robust, it is academia. But that is not the world described by this history professor, whose identity was vouched for by Wilfred Reilly, an assistant professor at historically black Kentucky State University.

The letter highlights the absence of diversity of opinion on the topic of anti-police protests in department emails. They pledge diversity while offering none, according to the writer. The author complains that the department recognizes only one problem in the black community: white people. They provide links and documentation of this argument "to the near exclusion of all others" to make the case that "the problems of the black community are caused by whites," without "a single counter-argument to their prevailing narrative." So the writer offers one.

> The ever-present soft bigotry of low expectations and the permanent claim that the solutions to the plight of my people rest exclusively on the goodwill of whites rather than on our own hard work is psychologically devastating. No other group in America is systematically demoralized in this way by its alleged allies. A whole generation of black children are being taught that only by begging and weeping and screaming will they get handouts from guilt-ridden whites.

The author objects to the notion that black lives matter only when whites take them, saying these views are in themselves racist. They essentially argue that black violence is expected while white violence requires explanation and demands solution. "Please look into your hearts and see how monstrously bigoted this formulation truly is," the author writes. The letter then takes issue with the "condescending depredations" of the Democratic

Party, which assumes that "we [black people] are too stupid to do STEM, that we need special help and lower requirements to get ahead in life. I sometimes wonder if it wouldn't be easier to deal with open fascists, who at least would be straightforward in calling me a subhuman, and who are unlikely to share my race," the writer says.

The response by the University of California, Berkeley is telling. They write, unironically:

> An anonymous letter has been circulating, purportedly written by a @UCBHistory professor. We have no evidence that this letter was written by a History faculty member. We condemn this letter: it goes against our values as a department and our commitment to equity and inclusion.

Constitutional law professor Jonathan Turley, who takes issue with some of the content of the letter, nevertheless expresses great concern about the implications of this response on free speech and academic freedom in America. He writes, "What concerns me is that Berkeley's response notably does not even bother to state the pretense of tolerance for opposing views. The condemnation would seem to reaffirm rather than redress the concerns over academic freedom and free speech for dissenting faculty members."

The pressure within academia to cater to leftist narratives came into sharp focus after authors of a study that went against the police brutality narrative retracted it. Not because the data was faulty or the conclusions wrong, but because the objective facts the study revealed suddenly became inconvenient to the leftist political narrative. The 2019 study, which had appeared in a peer-reviewed journal, concluded that black people were not being shot by police at disparate rates when compared to other races. After the study was cited in a congressional hearing, Michigan

State University demoted physicist Steve Hsu, who didn't author the study, but who approved funding to even research the topic. Subsequently, authors Joseph Cesario of Michigan State and David Johnson of the University of Maryland retracted the study, claiming the data had been "misused."

Cancel Culture Comes for the Doctors

Even in medicine, people whose views veer from the leftist narrative are not safe. In late July, frontline doctors gathered in Washington, D.C., for a "white coat summit" to address misinformation about COVID-19. These were a diverse group of practicing physicians currently treating patients with the disease.

Clips from the conference went viral, amassing eighteen million views before Facebook, YouTube, and Twitter pulled the video, claiming it contained "misinformation" about the virus. Facebook removed a livestream that had fifteen million views. Twitter forced participating doctors to delete their own video testimonials. The group's website was taken down with a claim that doctors had violated the providers' terms of service by publicizing their experience-based medical opinions. The doctors' speech was labeled too dangerous for public consumption.

The media focused almost exclusively on the bizarre religious beliefs of Cameroonian American Stella Immanuel, a Houston doctor educated in Nigeria who gave a spirited defense of hydroxychloroquine.

Though some physicians and claims during that event were more credible than others, the experience and conclusions of these doctors belong in the debate on this issue. If they are wrong, let them be defeated by the facts, not the censors.

In the video, doctors made claims that hydroxychloroquine

worked both as a prophylactic to prevent the virus and as a treatment in combination with other drugs. PolitiFact, in disputing the claims made, argued the video "disputes the claims of public health experts." But public health experts have themselves been purveyors of misinformation. No one has suggested censoring them, firing them, or taking down websites. Public health experts told us in January the virus was "not a major threat." In February, Surgeon General Jerome Adams tweeted, "Seriously people—STOP BUYING MASKS!" They got the mortality rate wrong, the death toll, the modeling, the projections of how many ventilators would be needed. In June, the World Health Organization (WHO) told us there was no asymptomatic transmission of the virus, then reversed course a day later.

But for describing the real-world impact of an inexpensive drug that has been safely prescribed for six decades, frontline doctors who are certainly qualified to make medical recommendations were silenced. Even if they were wrong—and time will tell if they were—why was their advice any more dangerous than the CDC telling America "if you are NOT sick you do not need to wear a facemask unless you are caring for someone who is sick." In their fact check of the claims made by the doctors, PolitiFact echoed the argument used by many on the left to silence discussion of the drug—the research is not conclusive. Therefore it's dangerous to even talk about the treatment. Is that the standard? When has that standard ever been applied in public policy discussions of the efficacy of medical marijuana?

Within days, board-certified emergency physician Simone Gold, who had spent thirty-one years in the medical field, was fired from her job. Canceled. For publicly sharing medical advice she is perfectly qualified to share. Gold told Glenn Beck in a radio interview, "Most emergency physicians work at more than one [hospital], as I do, and I've actually been fired from both. They told me that I appeared in an embarrassing video, and therefore,

I would no longer be welcome to work there . . . then they said, if I didn't go quietly and I made a fuss, they would have all the doctors in the group, you know, they'd have to go and they'll get a whole new doctor group."

The drug she was promoting is not available over the counter. Patients can do little to act on her advice without the permission of a physician. Yet the CDC's advice on masks could have affected every American. This isn't about who is right. It's about who has rights.

Some on the left are beginning to recognize the path we're on. In an essay that infuriated fellow leftists, *Rolling Stone* journalist Matt Taibbi in June 2020 called out the cancel culture.

> It feels liberating to say after years of tiptoeing around the fact, but the American left has lost its mind. It's become a cowardly mob of upper-class social media addicts, Twitter Robespierres who move from discipline to discipline torching reputations and jobs with breathtaking casualness.

Published independently on Substack, the essay criticized ideas that Taibbi says are "so toxic and unattractive that they eschew debate, moving straight to shaming, threats, and intimidation."

Of the news industry's suppression of inconvenient narratives, Taibbi writes, "In a business where the first job requirement was once the willingness to ask tough questions, we've become afraid to ask obvious ones."

The threats to free speech are real. Leftists don't fear them because it's not their speech being suppressed. Sir Winston Churchill famously said, "Some people's idea of free speech is that they are free to say what they like, but if anyone says anything back, that is an outrage."

In the marketplace of ideas, the solution to bad speech is more speech. But how can ideas freely compete when whole perspectives are suppressed or misreported? Taibbi in his piece decried the lack of accountability in the media, concluding, "It's been learned in these episodes we may freely misreport reality, so long as the political goal is righteous."

CHAPTER 12

AN AMERICA WE DON'T RECOGNIZE

The list of constitutional rights we were asked to "temporarily" suspend during the crisis is long. We can still belong to our choice of faiths, but now the government has taken upon itself power to dictate the terms of our worship, leaving behind a Supreme Court precedent that will long outlast the virus. In many places, 2020 meant we could gather to burn Bibles, but not to teach from them.

Though we still technically have a free press, we have a media and technology sector actively practicing suppression of political narratives that breach progressive orthodoxy. Now content moderators and progressive CEOs have more say in what we can learn about medical treatments than the actual doctors who administer them. Leftists promote a future where we can neither own guns nor rely on police for protection—an agenda that will remain long after the virus disappears.

Frankly, it could have been a lot worse as far as civil liberties are concerned. We could have had a Democrat in the Oval Office. One who had just spent three years filling our courts with progressive judges who would happily use the pretext of a pandemic to rewrite the Constitution.

Of all the opportunities that might have presented themselves to a Democratic administration, among the most valuable politically might be the potential expansion of the surveillance state. We know how the Obama administration weaponized IRS data to shut down political groups during his second election, and how his FBI used surveillance data to entrap political adversaries and embroil them in baseless charges. Imagine what they could have done with access to our every physical move. Coronavirus provided a pretext for government to legitimately collect even more data than ever before. With President Trump at the helm, we didn't see a federal effort to capitalize on that opportunity. But it's important to understand what was at stake.

The Surveillance State Kicks into Gear

You could almost hear the enthusiasm of government bureaucrats churning out plans to "protect" the public from the pandemic's early stages. Imagine their delight at being able to monitor everyone, everywhere. They could dream of putting up drones to track us with facial recognition software, view our temperature via thermal imaging, scan our license plates if we try to gather together in a parking lot, and use apps on our phones to track our every movement. If we cross state lines, they can gather our information, use GPS to cross-reference those who get COVID-19 with others who cross our paths, and match that data with the FBI's database of citizens (which, I know firsthand, they have been developing in secret). They now had even more of a pretext to suppress "dangerous" social media postings, monitor our information flow, and track our credit card purchases.

Scary. At any other time in American history, such a package of proposals would set off alarms. But in the first half of 2020, as

COVID-19 was playing out and most of us were hunkered down in isolation, these ideas seemed almost reasonable. After all, they weren't coming from a tyrannical government bent on seizing more power, but from a benevolent bureaucracy looking to stem the tide of infectious disease. Some Americans simply accepted the incoming tide of heavy surveillance as the new normal. Without deep concern, and certainly without national debate, such invasive notions were accepted at face value with little mainstream analysis of the long-term ramifications. After all, it was working in Asia, wasn't it? To question them was considered unpatriotic, extremist, and anti-science.

Contact Tracing for Our Own Good

In April, all eyes were on Asia, where digital contact tracing was reportedly slowing the progression of the SARS-CoV-2 virus. Those nations had been hit harder by the SARS outbreak nearly two decades ago and had prepared to confront a similar outbreak. In Hong Kong, the government mandated residents wear electronic wrist bands that would track whether someone in quarantine had left their home. In Korea, emergency alerts would inform residents where an infected person had recently been. Results were promising. In one case, Bloomberg reported 9,000 people were tested based on a single infected person who went to a nightclub. The virus then jumped from the nightclub visitor, to a student, to a taxi driver, to a warehouse employee who had potentially exposed 4,000 people at the warehouse. With extensive testing and quarantines, the outbreak was reportedly limited to just 152 positive cases. It was an encouraging option in a world where a vaccine was still potentially years away.

Japan already had an army of trained contact tracers who did their work the old-fashioned way—with private interviews and individual contacts. That nation was able to successfully blunt the spread of the virus using existing public health infrastructure. China managed to keep the virus from infecting other cities to the degree that it infected Wuhan, if you believe their numbers. And Taiwan, ravaged in 2003 by the SARS outbreak, had a robust infrastructure in place that included digital contact tracing. That testing and infrastructure was largely credited for Taiwan's remarkable resistance to spread. By July 15, only 451 positive cases had been diagnosed among Taiwan's 24 million people.

Looking to Asia's success as a guide, states in May began hiring tens of thousands of contact tracers to prevent community spread. In theory, the activities of infected persons would be traced, either digitally or through personal interviews, and anyone else who might have been exposed could be quickly notified and quarantined. The CDC recommended 100,000 contact tracers would be needed.

It didn't quite work out as planned. By July 31 the *New York Times* declared the process was failing in many states. The reasons were predictable. There wasn't enough testing. Testing was too slow. Not enough people were participating. The virus became too ubiquitous too fast. It was expensive. According to the *Times*, few places have reported systemic success. New York City hired 3,000 contact tracers in May, but by June, the city reported tracers were having little success tracking down infected patients or getting them to share information. They were able to gather information on just 35 percent of the 5,347 city residents who tested positive or were presumed positive.

Former CDC director Thomas Frieden told the *New York Times* the number of cases was too high to make contact tracing effective. Frieden, whom the *Times* identified as a strong advocate for robust tracing programs, said, "At some point when your case counts are very high, you have to dial back your testing and contact tracing." But perhaps the biggest factor in the failure of contact tracing was the asymptomatic spread of the virus, which made identifying carriers nearly impossible.

So why did it work so much better in Asia? We still have a great deal to learn. But two reasons stand out. First, Asian people were willing to tolerate a greater degree of surveillance and restriction than Americans were. Second, many of the nations with the best success in combatting the virus were also hit hard by the SARS virus. Some research is beginning to suggest that patients who contracted SARS-CoV-1 seventeen years ago have developed a sort of T-cell response that inhibits SARS-CoV-2, which may explain why Asia's, and particularly Taiwan's, exposure to COVID-19 was so limited. Nevertheless, that research is still developing and remains theoretical as of this writing.

But what are the risks of sharing this much information? And what happens to all of that data when the crisis has passed? Loss of privacy may seem a small price to pay for saving lives, but the implications of empowering government to collect so much data about us are not without risk.

I have never seen a real-life genie outside of a bottle, but I am fairly certain once it gets out, it is difficult to put that genie back in. There is a reason that is a common saying. Give up some privacy to the government and good luck getting it back. Some may have felt safe at the outset, trusting those benevolent bureaucrats and corporate innovators to track us for our own good. But what happens if the bureaucrats and geniuses aren't so benevolent? What happens when our data becomes a commodity in the struggle for power? That's certainly a worthy concern, though one that is frequently dismissed as a conspiracy theory.

But a July 11 opinion piece in *The Hill* offered a glimpse of where contact tracing could take us. Northwestern University sociology professor Andrew Papachristos suggested contact tracing could serve a dual purpose. "The same techniques might be used to combat the public health epidemic of gun violence surging in recent weeks and months in cities across the U.S.," he wrote. He proposed applying a "model of contagion" to gun violence that would track the networks of shooters. "This sort of network data can produce information that can help violence prevention workers reach those at risk of exposure to harm." Government tracing of gun owners' every movement, the ability to notify others when a gun owner is nearby? As with so many leftist policy ideas, I find myself asking the question—*what could possibly go wrong?*

There is a more immediate concern that should give us pause as we consider how much access we give government to the data of our lives. Those people behind the data, who we're told are acting in our best interests, have a track record. And it is not good. I'm not talking about a history of malevolent activity so much as a history of carelessness and incompetence with private data.

The privacy concerns associated with contact tracing have been real, even in nations where the process has worked well. In South Korea, safety guidance texts revealed enough private information in some cases to allow people to connect the dots, identifying embarrassing private details and subjecting people to public criticism. Alerts have been detailed enough to fuel speculation about extramarital affairs or to bring down social stigma on their subjects. The *Guardian* newspaper described one alert that highlighted a man contracting the virus from an instructor during a sexual harassment class. Another reportedly involved a man in his fifties who had been to Wuhan, China, with his young secretary, where both were infected. The *Guardian* reports, "As South Korean media pored over their movements, citizens looked on with a mixture of horror and fascination as their private lives were laid bare, leading to speculation that they were having an affair and that the secretary had undergone plastic surgery."

Even when people are not identified, they can be subjected to derision and mockery online. The BBC reported on one alert in which a twenty-seven-year-old South Korean woman was identified as someone who worked at the Samsung plant in Gumi. After an alert revealed that she visited a friend who had attended a gathering of a religious sect where the virus had spread, panic ensued. The mayor revealed the woman's name in a Facebook post, leading to comments asking to know the name of her apartment building. According to the BBC, the woman begged for her privacy. BBC reported, "With most cases not leading to serious health problems, South Koreans now dread stigma as much as they fear the virus itself."

Trusting Government with Our Data

To understand the threat that giving government access to personal information poses, it's instructive to look at past data leak disasters.

As the incoming chairman of the House Oversight Committee, I had the prerogative to reorganize the committee structure. I created a new subcommittee in January 2015 specifically to conduct oversight of information technology. It was an issue many members of Congress and many bureaucrats did not understand. I felt it required greater scrutiny than Congress had been able to provide. Little did I know, one of the most dangerous security breaches in government history had already taken place.

Not until several months later did we learn of the massive data breach at the Office of Personnel Management (OPM). The sensitive security clearance information of more than 21 million people had been exfiltrated in a series of breaches going back more than a year, presumably at the direction of the Chinese government. How did they manage to hack into such sensitive records? It wasn't that hard.

OPM had failed to implement basic security measures, including two-factor authentication, which would have prevented someone with a stolen username and password (the first authentication) from accessing the system without a chip-enhanced ID card (the second authentication). Apparently anyone with access to an active username and password could get in.

Despite the negative publicity surrounding the OPM breach, other government agencies remained complacent. In November of that same year, we learned from the inspector general for the Department of Education that data for 40 million federal student loan borrowers was not secure. We learned the department was using technology that was not even supported at the time. We learned they had 139 million unique Social Security numbers in the department's Central Processing System, but had not heeded warnings from the inspector general to lock it down.

The most massive government breach was yet to come. In December 2015, 198 million voter records, including personal information on every American voter, were left exposed to the open internet by a government contractor. The database containing names, dates of birth, emails, addresses, and party affiliation for registered voters in all fifty states and Washington, D.C., was improperly configured, leaving data exposed.

That was just the first year of the new subcommittee's existence. Unfortunately, that subcommittee no longer exists. Democrats dismantled it when they won the majority in 2018, in favor of a new Civil Rights and Civil Liberties Subcommittee ostensibly aimed at protecting freedom of speech, religion, and assembly. I kid you not. Given how little interest that subcommittee took in the COVID-19-related incursions of civil liberties, the trade-off was not a good one for the American people.

Nevertheless, the experience of the short-lived information

technology oversight effort revealed reasons to be cautious. At the heart of the government surveillance problem is the inability of a large, slow, sclerotic bureaucracy to stay on the cutting edge of cybersecurity technology. Moving at the speed of technology is not the government's strong suit.

In a June 2019 survey from Pew Research, six months before COVID-19 surfaced, 64 percent of Americans reported they were somewhat or very concerned about government collection of their personal data. That's a high number, but it would likely be much higher if more Americans were paying attention to the government's track record of protecting their data.

As the subcommittee dug into the government's information technology systems, the news got more and more disturbing. We found agencies still using Windows 95 in 2015, courtesy of a slow procurement process that lagged far behind the technological expertise of the world's hackers. We found a competitive cybersecurity job market in which government was struggling to compete for top talent. We found subcontractors who had more current technology, but who had less control over who could actually access confidential records. There were vetting problems, cost overruns, and oversight issues with some of these government contractors.

The fact is, government is not structured to move quickly enough to protect our data from hackers and foreign governments. Though we can't prevent government from collecting some data, we can embrace limited government to minimize what they can collect and store. As I learned during my time on the Oversight Committee, there seems to be no limit to the amount of data that government would like to collect. That propensity didn't start with COVID-19. But the pretext of the infectious disease would escalate it.

The FBI's Orwellian Facial Recognition Database

Without approval from Congress or disclosure to the American public, the FBI in 2010 began compiling a database of faces. Not the faces of convicted criminals. Not the faces of foreign visa holders. But the faces of law-abiding American citizens, many of whom are minors. Data is collected without their permission through state driver's license databases and other government sources.

At the time, I was alarmed as I considered hypothetical applications for this technology. Those applications are no longer hypothetical. Since the public health crisis began, private companies have pitched the ability of "artificially intelligent thermal cameras" to be used in stores, airports, and corporate workplaces to detect fevers. But that's not all they do. China famously weaponized the technology to identify protesters in Hong Kong who could later be singled out for punishment.

The FBI's biometric database, called Next Generation Identification, was a souped-up version of the agency's fingerprint database developed in secret. Though required by law, the bureau did not publish a privacy impact statement for five years, when I learned of it in 2015.

I was livid. I learned that approximately half of adult Americans at the time had their photographs stored in that database, where they could be accessed without their knowledge or permission. Noncriminal entries make up about 80 percent of photos in the FBI's network, sourced from driver's licenses and passports. Even more disturbing, I discovered that the algorithms used to identify matches are wrong 15 percent of the time. Even worse, they are more likely to misidentify black people than white people.

The FBI argued in a public hearing before the House Oversight Committee that the database enhances their ability to solve crimes and that it is used primarily to generate investigative leads. No doubt that's true. But just because a violation of civil liberties makes crime fighting easier doesn't mean we should embrace it.

For example, it would be easier to solve crimes if we collected everyone's DNA at birth, kept hair samples, fingerprints, etc. It would be easier to get criminals off the streets if we didn't have to stop and read people their *Miranda* rights or go through a process of discovery. But we don't do those things. It's an invasion of our civil rights as well as our privacy. The government has to show probable cause—or at least articulable suspicion—before they can collect our DNA or our fingerprints. As a suspicionless American, you get to live your life without having to carry papers with you or have your DNA in some government database. It looks cool on-screen when Jack Bauer of the TV show *24* accesses all those rich government databases. But this isn't Hollywood. Collecting all of that data doesn't necessarily make us safer.

When we learned of the FBI database in 2015, the horrified response from Congress was bipartisan. My colleague Democrat representative Stephen Lynch of Massachusetts said at the time, "This is really Nazi Germany here that we're talking about. They had meticulous files on individuals, most of them of Jewish faith, and that's how they tracked their people. I see little difference in the way people are being tracked under this."

What we didn't know then that we know now is that the FBI was at that very moment politicized. It was being run by Director James Comey, who would later stand accused of directing the use of the FBI apparatus to go after members of the incoming Trump administration. There would be documented cases of campaign surveillance, classified leaks, perjury traps, and unpredicated investigations. President Trump's pick for national security advisor, General Michael Flynn, would endure years of legal battles before the Trump administration would find and release the exculpatory information the FBI had withheld. Only then did the Justice Department drop the case against him.

This is the FBI that manages a database of faces, which they can access without showing probable cause. Bipartisan legislation introduced by Republican senator Mike Lee of Utah and Democratic senator Chris Coons of Delaware would require federal police agencies to obtain a warrant before accessing the database. Likewise, states like California are considering legislation to both enable the collection of data and simultaneously regulate the circumstances under which it can be accessed.

The FBI's facial recognition database was the forerunner to new technologies that could change Americans' expectation of privacy forever.

Government Surveillance Took Steroids in 2020

The data security and surveillance issues that concerned me in 2015 were small potatoes compared to what we began considering in 2020. Technology moves fast. The government's ability to surveil us has only grown.

When our son was little, one day we were at his grandmother's home in Mesa, Arizona. I remember twenty-plus years ago when he came running around the corner holding a vinyl record. He said, "Mom, Dad, look at this great big CD!" In his young life, he had only experienced CDs. In my kids' lifetime the pace of technological developments has occurred at an unimaginable speed. It seems everything is available and everything is at our fingertips for viewing. This obviously creates tremendous and unparalleled opportunities, but it also delivers unintended consequences.

In the months following the economic lockdown over

COVID-19, governments around the world sought to embrace the latest advances in surveillance tools to help with contact tracing during the global pandemic. *Wired* magazine reported countries green-lighting dragnet monitoring systems, seeking real-time location data from mobile providers, or deploying facial recognition. "These steps may usher in a long-term expansion of the surveillance state," they wrote in early April 2020. "Many democracies have tried, not always with success, to build legal barriers that constrain authorities' ability to access and exploit the personal information collected by private companies. Coronavirus surveillance could dismantle these structures."

Since then, we've seen the use of cell phone data, credit card histories, and thermal cameras to track people's personal movement. Some judges went so far as to order coronavirus patients to wear GPS ankle monitors to ensure they did not break quarantine. Such surveillance makes many uncomfortable—and it should.

When I was first elected to Congress in 2008, I attended a training meeting by the nonpartisan, nonprofit Congressional Institute. The organization hosts an array of orientation seminars for incoming members of Congress. At one particular session a very senior person from the National Security Agency (NSA) relayed some somber news. He told us that everything we had ever written or read on the internet had already been downloaded, archived, and probably analyzed by the various intelligence agencies around the world. My shocked reaction was—*yikes!*

The guy from the NSA was referring to non-USA intelligence agencies, but I have always wondered what kind of information is collected and stored by our own intelligence operations. Thor Benson is credited with writing, "Americans don't care about privacy, and the people running the country couldn't be happier." It does make you think, because as author Stephen King wrote, "No one likes to see a government folder with his name on it."

Just because it can be done, doesn't mean we should be doing it. And I simply don't trust the federal government. The Fourth Amendment reads,

> The right of the people to be secure in their persons, houses, papers, and effects, against unreasonable searches and sei-zures, shall not be violated, and no warrants shall issue, but upon probable cause, supported by oath or affirmation, and particularly describing the place to be searched, and the per-sons or things to be seized.

Before the United States of America was the United States of America, the British had general warrants called writs of assis-tance. Our Fourth Amendment was created to protect the people from the overarching ways of a government as our Founders had experienced firsthand. It helped enforce the doctrine where "each man's home is his castle."

Interestingly, it starts with, "The right of the people to be se-cure in their persons . . ." Without diving deep into case law and analysis, suffice it to say the Fourth Amendment does far more than simply protect you at home in your castle. As William O. Douglas argued in *Public Utilities Commission v. Pollak* in 1952, "The right to be let alone is indeed the beginning of all freedom."

I don't mean to ever belittle or diminish the very real con-cerns and fright any one of the array of issues posing a threat to our lives brings to us. I thoroughly understand and relate to the fear driving so many to willingly forgo privacy, but I do hope we collectively think through and understand the unintended consequences and long-term ramifications because our younger generations are experiencing advancements in technological ca-pabilities at warp speed, and not all are for the best.

"They who can give up essential liberty to obtain a little

temporary safety deserve neither liberty nor safety," said Benjamin Franklin, one of America's brightest.

The Trade-Offs of Liberty

One of the reasons China is credited with acting so quickly and successfully to stem the tide of coronavirus within its borders is that the central government controls so many levers of power. There are no privacy concerns. No guarantees of free speech, assembly, or press to worry about. There is no independent state and local government apparatus. All is controlled by the CCP. In China, one size has to fit all.

And that's the trade-off. A July 2020 analysis from Australia's Lowy Institute, a public policy think tank, suggested that modern democracies could not hope to replicate China's response to the virus. Without any "messy, democratic debate about civil rights and so forth," they write, the government was able to lock down more than 700 million people in residential detention—and to do it virtually overnight. It was also able to seal borders at every level, shut down businesses, commandeer resources, mobilize the military, and mandate testing and tracking, according to the analysis. A government that can do those things at that speed can do a great many other things that we may not support. Indeed, China operates concentration camps, for which prisoners qualify based on a religious test. Uighur Muslims and Falun Gong practitioners automatically qualify. For the broader population, China surveils social media use and doles out privileges on the basis of political and social compliance. It is not compelled to honor due process, as many in the once-free city-state of Hong Kong are experiencing firsthand.

Those impediments to federal power are what have protected

the U.S. from becoming more like China. Yet today's Democratic Party is demanding we act more like China. Nancy Pelosi has made her position crystal clear. In a May 25 tweet thread, Pelosi criticized President Trump's failure to seize power in a crisis, writing, "The Trump Administration still does not have a serious plan to increase testing," claiming his plan was to "reject responsibility and dump the burden on to the states."

CHAPTER 13

THE MEMORY HOLE

With the election of Donald Trump in 2016, I looked forward to the restoration of checks and balances on the power of the president that had lain dormant for eight long years. One check was a free press.

The press was technically free during the Obama administration. But mainstream outlets voluntarily functioned as a propaganda arm of the progressive movement. They were asleep at the wheel because they fawned over Barack Obama. In my experience, it didn't matter what scandal surfaced, major outlets weren't going to report on it in a fair and impartial way. I know that to be the case because I saw the scandals and corruption on one side, and the total lack of enthusiasm and intellectual curiosity on the other side. Interest in these issues should have been pervasive within the Beltway, as it had during other administrations before and since.

I naïvely hoped they would call balls and strikes as they saw them. But that wasn't happening under either administration. During the Obama administration, they functioned as a lapdog for the president. During the Trump administration, they became opposition research for the Democratic Party.

Sure, there were conservative outlets at that time doing the heavy lifting to report stories the mainstream press dismissed. But unlike conservative voters, who are daily confronted with the narratives of the opposing party across media, culture, and sports, progressive voters and many moderate voters have no such exposure. If mainstream sources don't report facts that go against the narratives, these voters never see them. Conservative sources get demonized, mocked, and censored and are thus easily avoided. Many voters only see the facts mainstream outlets want them to see while inconvenient narratives get ignored and censored. Or, too often, they get shoved down the memory hole, to be incinerated and forgotten as the narrative shifts and the goalposts move.

Seeing these tactics at work during the previous administration was one thing. That was about politics. But seeing them play out during a global pandemic, an outbreak of nationwide protests and violence, and an economic lockdown raised the stakes even higher. The ease with which certain facts could be dispatched, hidden, or memory-holed became an even greater liability for a nation dependent on a free press to inform representative government.

There is a proper role for legitimate journalism in our country. We want a strong segment of the media that is balanced, impartial, and unbiased. Even among outlets that reflect a certain perspective, we depend on a commitment to truth, justice, and fair representations of opposing points of view. We saw little of that during the Obama years. To this day, many still peddle the lie that the biggest scandal of that administration was President Obama's decision to wear a tan suit.

It simply wasn't the truth. Not only were there scandals, but there were red flags everywhere that the federal government apparatus was being weaponized for political warfare to a degree this nation had never seen before. But the media was curiously incurious.

I speak from firsthand experience. During the entirety of the Obama administration, I had a seat on the House Oversight Committee, where it was my job to investigate the scandals, the corruption, and the incompetence that needed to be exposed and rooted out. Not all of it was malicious. Not all of it was made public.

Government is large. With 2.2 million employees, I often say there is always going to be someone doing something stupid somewhere. But some of what we uncovered was legitimately corrupt, dishonest, or illegal. I saw firsthand the complete disinterest in any story that might be harmful to the interests of the left.

I had the privilege of serving not only as a committee member, but as chairman of the House Oversight and Government Reform Committee under both President Obama and President Trump. The contrast between the media interest in oversight work during the Obama administration (limited) and the Trump administration (voracious) was vast. Let me share one example.

I remember a particularly newsworthy story in the final year of the Obama administration that should have been front-page news all around the world. Under a Trump administration, it clearly would have been. It was September 2016 and we had just learned that Obama's FBI director, James Comey, and the Department of Justice had granted immunity from prosecution to five people very close to Hillary Clinton, including Clinton's chief of staff, Cheryl Mills.

It was a big story for several reasons. First, neither Comey nor Attorney General Loretta Lynch had disclosed it to Congress when asked. Second, the government inexplicably offered immunity from prosecution and asked for absolutely nothing in return. And third, the existence of immunity agreements ensured none of the key witnesses in the Clinton case had to cooperate with congressional investigations, essentially ensuring that the truth would never be fully known.

I had questioned Comey directly in a public hearing months

earlier about whether there were any immunity agreements in place. He had to know there were five of them in place. But he feigned ignorance and said he had to check. Months later, when we finally forced the hand of the DOJ, they only gave us three, omitting the two most explosive ones. At the end of the meeting when I asked if this was all of them, the presenter sheepishly admitted there were others. I became frustrated and demanded they produce them immediately.

A few days later they brought them to us. Representatives John Ratcliffe and Trey Gowdy, both former federal prosecutors, were stunned by what they read. There was no requirement for the immunity recipients to cooperate with the government. They were protected from prosecution without having to give the government any information at all. For those involved in these types of agreements previously, this was an astounding revelation. What would be the purpose of offering immunity if you expect to get nothing in return? Mills was a witness as well as a potential target of the investigation. Yet Comey had inexplicably agreed not to prosecute Mills for anything he might find on her laptop regarding the contents of Hillary Clinton's secret classified emails. And because of her immunity agreement, she and the others could thumb their nose at Congress or a subsequent Justice Department without fear of legal repercussions.

This was a huge story.

Knowing of a specific reporter at a major newspaper who had actually done some digging on related stories, I reached out to him first after discovering the disturbing news. I wanted word to get out. The public had a right to know. This was not acceptable. The reporter was elated to be the first to get the story. He needed to talk to his editor. Then he'd get right back to me.

I waited. And waited. Finally, I had to be the one to call him back. They would not be running the story, he told me apologetically. He regretted to tell me that his editor didn't feel it was newsworthy. Not newsworthy? It was a stunning revelation.

But it was negative to the candidate the outlet had glowingly covered—Hillary Clinton. Instead of pursuing a legitimate story and writing it, they suppressed it. It's possible they may have buried some mention of the revelation deep in a carefully framed story somewhere, but it never merited a headline. Fortunately, the Associated Press ended up writing the story and it did ultimately get picked up by some mainstream outlets.

With the election of Donald Trump, no negative story was too insignificant. No source too lacking in credibility. No story too wild to be told. I had tried to tell myself that maybe having the media finally wake up would be a positive development. At least the executive branch would have another source of oversight. But it didn't quite work out that way.

What happened during the Trump administration was a media unleashed against the president, untethered to the truth, and largely unaccountable for the false narratives it so eagerly spread. With help from their friends in the tech sector and like-minded celebrities, even the most outrageous false claims against the Trump administration spread rapidly. Media could "report" anything they wanted about Donald Trump and it was immediately and uncritically accepted. When the truth finally emerged some twenty-four or forty-eight hours later (or in the case of FISA abuses and Russian collusion, years later), the damage was done. The original false reporting was memory-holed. No one was held to account.

False narratives are not new. Biased reporting is not new. What is new is the degree to which like-minded politicians, media, and tech companies work in tandem to control the flow of false stories and prevent the dissemination of true ones. We expect the media to vet things. But that wasn't happening during the Trump administration. The tendency to accept uncritically any tidbit of information, no matter how tenuous the source, was rampant. Two years after the 2016 election, a YouGov poll found 67 percent of Democrats still believed the baseless claim that "Russia tampered with vote tallies in order to get Donald Trump elected." There was never a shred of evidence that vote tallies themselves were manipulated. It wasn't even credibly alleged. Yet two-thirds of Democrats believed the narrative.

The coverage upholding leftist narratives often appears synchronized, with every outlet seeming to use coordinated words and phrases at the same time. In June, the common phrase was "peaceful protest"—a depiction that was seldom used during nonviolent lockdown protests the previous month. When old narratives become unfavorable, such as the notion that President Trump had overreacted to the virus by shutting down travel from China, those stories quickly disappear, replaced by the new narrative that President Trump didn't act fast enough. For anyone paying attention to facts, it can be dizzying.

Which is why social media has been such a game changer—and why the power to censor it has become such a cultural touchpoint. It's why Donald Trump used social media so successfully. It provided a forum to bypass the media gatekeepers and disseminate information they would prefer people didn't know. During the pandemic, unchecked media narratives were a particularly useful tool for the left. They spread misinformation far and wide with little accountability. When a claim is too good to be true, it spreads like wildfire, even without evidence. But go back in light of later developments and see if you can find the news story acknowledging the previous errors. You might find something buried at the bottom of a "news" story with a provocative headline heralding a leftist narrative. But a mea culpa can be hard to come by.

Recall what happened immediately after the violence began to break out in Minneapolis. The video footage of looting and stores set on fire was so horrifying that leftists began to speculate that it must obviously be Trump supporters behind the worst of it. Media outlets ran with the narrative on the flimsiest of evidence. It seems ridiculous now, as the protests spread to so many cities and the events of Portland and Seattle made denial of organized leftist involvement impossible. But in the early days, the narrative was prevalent.

The liberal media's early reports of white supremacists secretly infiltrating the "peaceful protests" to make them look bad have been lost down the memory hole. In July, Richmond, Virginia, mayor Levar Stoney told the *Virginia Mercury News* that it was white supremacists who "spearheaded" violence in his city. But when pressed, police acknowledged they had evidence only that some men in Hawaiian shirts and presumably associated with the boogaloo movement were "spotted in the crowd and denounced by other marchers," according to the *Mercury News*. When the outlet asked police to elaborate, Police Chief Gerald Smith reportedly replied that it was "certainly spoken of on social media outlets."

By that time, the story of white supremacists had gone viral, and of course, that reporting didn't get amplified nearly to the extent of the original allegations. The closest thing to evidence of white supremacist involvement is a Minneapolis case in which police identified the man who became known as "umbrella man." He was recorded carrying an umbrella while smashing store windows at an AutoZone. Police never charged or identified the man publicly, but they said he was affiliated with a white supremacist group called the Aryan Cowboys. There is no evidence to suggest the man was part of a larger effort to incite rioting.

In Las Vegas, Nevada, three men with links to a white supremacist group were arrested for conspiring to do something they didn't manage to carry out. Not good—but hardly a smoking gun for the narrative that nationwide violence was sparked by white supremacists. There was a white supremacist Twitter account with a few hundred followers that had to be shut down after it impersonated an Antifa group and invited violence in the suburbs. But that's about the extent of the evidence.

You can still easily find those original stories blaming Trump supporters for instigating violence at the riots. But good luck finding any story that explicitly corrects the record or holds the media accountable for spreading this evidence-free narrative, which I was still seeing repeated months later. As of this writing, tens of thousands have been arrested at various riots, but I can count on one hand the number of arrests that involve someone suspected of being tied to white supremacy.

The subheading of an article at NBC News on May 30 read, "Minnesota Gov. hints that white supremacists, drug cartels could be part of widespread chaos." The outlet reported that Governor Tim Walz was "aware of unconfirmed reports that gangs of white supremacists are taking advantage of the anarchy unfolding in Minneapolis to create chaos." Minneapolis mayor Jacob Frey chimed in, tweeting the same day, "We are now confronting white supremacists, members of organized crime, out of state instigators, and possibly even foreign actors to destroy and destabilize our city and our region." Walz went so far as to justify federal intervention in the riots because "the cartels, who are wondering if there was a break in their drug transmissions, are trying to take advantage of the chaos. That's why this is on a federal level." I guess the idea of federal intervention was less offensive when they thought the violence was coming from political adversaries. I don't doubt Walz and Frey were sincere in their belief that the violence must be coming from the Trump side of politics. But it simply wasn't true.

Senator Mazie Hirono amplified this view of the situation before Congress, saying, "President Trump has ignored factual evidence showing that white supremacists have hijacked peaceful protests to incite violence and stoke racial conflict, such as in Minneapolis."

Soon, MSNBC's Joy Reid chimed in, without evidence, to spread the unfounded allegations. "This is who's burning Minneapolis," she wrote optimistically, retweeting the NBC story, "not the protesters who are grieving George Floyd." The thread went on to share what Reid said she heard from Minnesota officials, "that white nationalist groups are planning online, to blend into the protests and stir chaos." She then questions, "What logical reason would LEFTwing groups have to burn black communities?"

Indeed.

Reid went on to explain what was really happening in Minneapolis, in her view. "Use your common sense, and calmly reason through what you are seeing. And keep in mind who the Trump regime is," she wrote. Of course. The violence had to be the fault of President Trump. It couldn't be the left, or burn-it-all nihilists, or criminal opportunists. For disaster liberalism to be invoked, the riots had to be blamed on white supremacists, who in turn had to be portrayed as agents of President Trump.

Amplified by news outlets across the country, the white supremacist lie was an article of faith before the weekend was out. May 30 also saw *Vice* reporting, "Far-right extremists are hoping to turn the George Floyd protests into a new civil war."

Pulitzer Prize winner and historian Nikole Hannah-Jones, creator of the 1619 Project revision of American history, also responded to the claims made without evidence.

Whew. Folks on here clearly need to read up on the long history of how the FBI and other counterintelligence groups infiltrate black protest movements to cause chaos and turn popular support, as well as how white supremacist groups still infiltrate law enforcement.

See. We don't even need facts or evidence. We just need to see history through the eyes of Nikole Hannah-Jones to know what really happened.

A few days later, when retired African American police captain David Dorn was murdered by looters in St. Louis, filmmaker Tariq Nasheed was quick to assign blame. "He was most likely shot by white supremacists (or, as you say, 'very fine people') who are infiltrating these protests," he tweeted, again, without evidence.

Nasheed was wrong. By June 8, police would arrest twenty-four-year-old African American Stephan Cannon for first-degree murder in the case. Cannon, by all accounts, is not a white supremacist. Rather, he is a convicted felon who served not a day of a 2014 seven-year sentence for felony robbery. Local television station Fox 2 Now reported Cannon received suspended execution of sentence (SES) in St. Louis, after which he violated parole twice and still never went to prison. Cannon was presumably not looting over the fact that the criminal justice system had been unfair to him.

Despite the sounding off of liberal commentators (Reza Aslan, and Seth Abramson, for example) on Twitter, there is no evidence Trump supporters initiated the wanton destruction at the CNN Center on May 29 and 30. Though Trump supporters certainly have more motive to attack CNN than Black Lives Matter does, it didn't actually turn out that way. Video evidence seems to clearly show a preponderance of black protesters throwing projectiles at police and demanding change. Of course, you won't find a news story clearing that up. It's difficult to imagine there was hard evidence of a vast right-wing conspiracy to attack CNN headquarters that somehow went unnoticed by—CNN. President Trump used Twitter to set the narrative straight, writing, "In an ironic twist of fate, CNN HQ is being attacked by the very riots they promoted as noble & just."

As Attorney General Bill Barr addressed media that day to call out far-left Antifa groups involved in the protests, left-wing journalists tweeted their disgust that Barr didn't repeat the white supremacy narratives coming out of Minnesota. A May 30 tweet from radio host and journalist Michelangelo Signorile: "Bill Barr on TV now saying the violence and rioting is coming from 'far-left,' 'Antifa' without any evidence. No evidence, took no questions. But in fact, MN govt officials are saying it is white supremacist and right-wing groups, per their investigations, evidence." I guess evidence is only required when the left is being accused. As for the so-called evidence coming out of Minnesota? Underwhelming.

Governor Walz had started out referencing unconfirmed reports. He had then argued foreign actors, drug cartels, and out-of-state protesters were responsible for the violence. He had told reporters that state officials had said 80 percent of protesters in Minneapolis came from outside the state. But of the fifty-seven people actually arrested by Saturday morning of that first violent weekend, forty-seven were residents of Minnesota. The *Washington Post* tried to find evidence for the drug cartel claims, but came up empty. "A federal law enforcement official was not aware of any intelligence about cartels infiltrating the protests," they wrote late on May 30. Still, the lack of evidence didn't stop a narrative that was just too good to be true.

Commentator Jonathan Chait, who writes for *New York* magazine, also furthered the wishful thinking, writing on June 1, "One sign that liberals shouldn't be defending antifa is that it's literally impossible to distinguish them from white supremacist militias right now," implying that such militias were rampant. He added, "By 'literally' I mean: every demonstration has some violent white men undermining their work, and they're either antifa or white supremacists, and nobody is exactly sure which." He was half right. The subsequent protests around the country would see large numbers of white people participating, using racism as the springboard to draw attention to a host of other political issues. But for the most part, they would be white liberals using racism as a pretext for their calls for Medicare-for-All, Green New Deal legislation, and vote-by-mail elections.

If Chait was right, and there were so many white supremacists starting riots in so many cities at the same time, the Southern Poverty Law Center would have been busy tracking it all. After all, monitoring such groups is the main reason they exist. Just one problem. There was little to track. Buried twenty-eight paragraphs deep in a May 31 *New York Times* story on the allegations that right-wing extremists infiltrated riots was this quote from Southern Poverty Law Center research analyst Howard Graves. Graves is responsible for tracking white supremacist groups. He told the *New York Times*, "I have not seen any clear evidence that white supremacists or militiamen are masking up and going out to burn and loot." Ouch.

In fact, there is very little evidence that the actions of white supremacist groups had any impact on the riots at all, outside of a few isolated incidents, several of which remain unsubstantiated as of this writing. The left must know it. Otherwise, why wouldn't they want mass arrests at these protests? If they really believed white supremacists were behind the violence, they wouldn't have defended them.

Given the widespread reporting of white supremacists and Trump supporters driving the violence at these riots, one might expect to find a mea culpa somewhere. Good luck. The whole scenario went down the memory hole. We're all supposed to forget the certainty with which our pundits and politicians assured us the far right drove the violence. We're supposed to forget that some of the protesters were also looters. Right-wing protests can be defined by the one guy (allegedly) holding a sign with a swastika, but left-wing protests require us to magically forget the fourteen thousand people arrested for potentially violating the law. That's how many people the *Washington Post* reported were arrested just between May 27 and June 12. No doubt had there been a mass of Trump supporters among that number, the *Post* would have breathlessly reported it. The leftists at *The Nation* tell us that "the fate of these protesters is in the hands of prosecutors. If those prosecutors want to be on the right side of history, they must not reinforce the same structures and institutions that the protesters and racial justice movement seeks to dismantle. They should drop the charges." Obviously, *The Nation* wouldn't have called for such a response had they believed white Trump supporters or white supremacists were truly behind the violence, would they?

COVID-19 Mistakes

A similar pattern emerges when we look at the narratives surrounding COVID-19 and the mistakes made in trying to contain it. Despite the monster numbers of people who died unnecessarily in New York and New Jersey, the narrative peddled by the left placed more blame on President Trump and red state mayors in electorally significant states like Florida and Georgia. What really went wrong?

Had one state, New York, implemented social distancing measures just two weeks earlier, former CDC head Tom Frieden said, we could have reduced New York's death toll by up to 80 percent. The virus in New York City, where subways remained open and crowded, then went on to become the primary source of infections across the country. New York cases fueled outbreaks in Louisiana, Texas, Arizona, and the West Coast, according to reporting from the *New York Times*. Geneticists tracked signature mutations of the virus to identify its origins. "During crucial weeks in March," the *Times* reported, "New York's political leaders waited to take aggressive action, even after identifying hundreds of cases, giving the virus a head start."

A second, perhaps more deadly mistake by at least five state governors caused the virus to spread through nursing homes. Ignoring federal protocols, five governors mandated that COVID-positive patients be sent back to their nursing homes to recover. The intent was to clear hospital capacity. But the result unleashed the deadly contagion among its most vulnerable targets. New York governor Andrew Cuomo's mandate resulted in at least 6,200 nursing home deaths as the virus spread through facilities unprepared to take on the disease. That number didn't include anyone who got sick in a nursing home and subsequently died in a hospital.

That policy was repeated by five other blue state governors, including New Jersey's Phil Murphy, Michigan's Gretchen Whitmer, California's Gavin Newsom, and Pennsylvania's Tom Wolf.

By the end of June, almost half of all COVID-19 deaths were in the state of New York. The death rate at that time was 5 percent, except in nursing homes, where it was an astounding 17 percent. Eleven percent of all COVID deaths nationally were in nursing homes or long-term care centers. But two weeks later, Governor Cuomo was taking a victory lap. As cases peaked and then dropped, Cuomo claimed to have turned the corner, plateaued the mountain, and come down on the other side. Even more baffling was the praise of Dr. Anthony Fauci, who heads the administration's virus response, saying New York "did it correctly." We were all supposed to forget about the nursing homes. Down the memory hole went that narrative. Left-wing media moved on to talk about spikes in southern states that, measured against Cuomo's massive death count, were relatively small.

By the end of July, at least 62,000 residents and workers of long-term care facilities around the country had died from the coronavirus, and 362,000 had been infected there, according to a *New York Times* database. More than 40 percent of U.S. coronavirus deaths were linked to long-term care facilities, either from patients or staff.

Fox News head meteorologist Janice Dean knows this story well. Both of her in-laws died of COVID-19 in New York during the pandemic. Her father-in-law died alone in a nursing home, where he contracted the virus and then was locked down. Weeks later, her mother-in-law died at home from the virus; neither received a funeral.

Dean wondered why no one seems interested in talking about Cuomo's role in those nursing home deaths. On a July 2020 interview on *The Guy Benson Show*, Dean explained her frustration with media refusal to hold Cuomo accountable for his disastrous policies.

> [T]his is why I am curious, and this is why I have gone to social media to scream as loud as I can because no one else will cover it. He [Cuomo] goes on GMA for a two-part interview. He doesn't even go near the nursing home question. This nursing home issue has killed 6,000 in New York. This should be one of the biggest scandals this state has ever seen under this governor. And no one asked the question. Wolf Blitzer didn't ask him a couple of days ago on CNN. I've been watching these interviews, and that's why I'm so furious. If this was a Republican governor, it would be on every page of every mainstream newspaper. On every single network. and it's not there. And people don't know about it. And that's why I'm furious.

The failures in New York were substantial. They were systemic. They deserve scrutiny and analysis. No doubt progressives can point to what they believe were failures of the Trump administration in addressing the virus. But there is no lack of coverage of that debate. Even the false claims, such as the notion that public health experts always advised us to wear masks, or that President Trump advised people to inject themselves with bleach, continue to get amplified. But when it comes to blue state mistakes, it's time to open the memory hole.

The Fight for Truth

Meanwhile, efforts to get to the truth and amplify it were simply not picked up by mainstream media outlets. These claims of white supremacist origins for the widespread rioting were made and amplified, then there was virtually no follow-up when the truth conflicted with the narrative.

We all play an important role in supporting the dissemination of facts and truth. The business model under which journalism operates has changed. As print advertising has become virtually extinct, subscribers are more important than ever. We vote with our feet. Are we willing to pay to support journalism we trust? Do we amplify the stories that get the facts right or share a perspective we believe in? We don't have to immerse ourselves in politics all the time. But when we do, where do we choose to direct our attention and the attention of those we can influence?

There are top-notch publications doing yeoman's work to cover the narratives being dismissed by the mainstream media. There are independent journalists disseminating quality work on podcasts, on Twitter, and on their own independent websites. I've cited some of their work in this book. But if you want to find the best coverage, you have to look for it. When seeking information, look to alternative search engines. I can't tell you the difference I get in results between Google and DuckDuckGo or a more conservative-oriented search engine like searchconservative.com. There is still a place for those mainstream sources. But we have to learn to look beyond them as well to get to the facts they choose not to share with us.

Just because the Justice Department inspector general issues a damning report confirming the spying of the Obama administration on the Trump campaign doesn't mean media outlets will highlight the most damning parts. Just because violence and vandalism were a nightly occurrence in Portland during the Black Lives Matter protests doesn't mean the media will stop portraying those protests as peaceful. Just because the long-term impact of the summer protests continues to negatively affect inner-city black lives and livelihoods doesn't mean you'll read about those impacts in the *Washington Post*.

Many so-called straight news publications don't pick up those inconvenient stories. Or they consign the narrative-busting information to the last paragraphs of the story. The media has come to realize they can lie, they can misinform, they can exaggerate and their side—the side with which they not-so-secretly politically align—will not expose them for it. Their allies in the tech sector will ensure only the most helpful narratives get boosted. Social media sites will help them suppress inconvenient narratives. They can perpetuate a story line for further shock value—click bait—with scant support and get away with it.

The press is still technically free, but only approved narratives are being amplified. The combined efforts of media, technology, and political groups have created a Ministry of Truth for the modern age. For stories that go against the leftist narrative, you have to dig to find them. Fortunately, more of us are learning how and where to dig.

ACKNOWLEDGMENTS

Life takes amazing twists and turns. Based on my grades in elementary and high school, nobody would have ever expected me to be writing books later in life. Oh, my teachers I am certain are shocked and bewildered. I certainly didn't show an interest in writing in my teenage years. My attention span was much shorter then. I would struggle staying focused on getting all the way through a Mad Libs back in the day. Now I am writing full books about how maddening the liberals are in life. Ha!

It took me a while to figure it out. I certainly don't have it all figured out, but I do now understand that life is a series of ups and downs, unexpected happenings, and opportunities that can fundamentally change the trajectory of your life. The trick is to not be paralyzed by the unanticipated being thrown at you on a daily, if not hourly, basis. Not everything is certain, and decisions are usually fraught with no clear answers. Often things happen to you that nobody could anticipate, such as an accident, a disease, or people letting you down by breaching a trust or breaking your heart.

For me, through the course of time, I learned to lean on personal prayer and a deep-seated belief in myself and my ability to make a decision. I knew whatever decision I made, I had to live with the decision and make the most of the decision. Whatever life threw at me, I simply had to deal with it. In my heart I knew I made the best possible choice I could at the time based on the information I had and the experiences I could draw upon.

This seems simple enough, but it never is that simple. For me it brings peace. Some situations are so difficult and seemingly insurmountable, but it is my experience you can get through them.

No matter what came my way, I was always grateful for the family and true friends around me to help me with the most mundane to the most devastating. Core to my life were my parents, both of whom have passed away, and my brother Alex, who joined the Chaffetz family when he was born three years, almost to the day, after me. I have leaned on him innumerable times through the good and bad. He has always been there for me and always will. For my mom, my dad, and my brother, Alex, I am eternally indebted.

In college I had the great fortune to see and later meet the love of my life, Julie. I love her, our three children, our son-in-law, our daughter-in-law, and our two grandchildren more than I ever could have imagined. Even after more than thirty years of marriage, life keeps getting better and better. The closeness I feel to my wife is something I cannot adequately express in words. To know me, you have to know Julie. She has always been supportive in every way. Running for Congress, being in Congress, and even life after Congress would not be possible without her. She is a great inspiration and I love her with all my heart.

So while I am gushing, please know I feel very blessed and fortunate to have been given the opportunity by HarperCollins Publishers, and their imprint Broadside Books, to write and have published my third book. I am most grateful you took the time to read it, or in many cases, listen to it. Your time and attention is valuable. Thank you for allowing me to share a perspective. I hope you found it illuminating.

The culmination of a complete book takes nearly a year of effort, starting with an editor who has the vision to understand what stories need to be told and captured in a book. Eric Nelson is at the top of his game and one of the best in the business. He understands the political climate and recognizes what would be of interest to the masses. In addition to his foresight, he is exceptionally easy and pleasant to work with as he guides a young writer through the process and coaches them through the minefield of potential problems. It takes mutual trust and collaboration to come up with a coherent, flowing book. Eric brings that all together.

Fortunately for me, my literary agent, David Larabell of Creative Artists Agency (CAA), brought me together with Eric Nelson. The first and second books, *Deep State* and then *Power Grab*, went exceptionally well, with both taking a spot on the *New York Times* bestseller list. They were full of congressional experiences and stories. Both were about my time in Congress, written from a perspective very few can relate to with firsthand knowledge. Book number three had to be a bit different. If I had a fascinating story from my time in Congress, and it didn't make it into the first two books, chances are it was either not that interesting or too salacious for what we were writing.

This book, as you now know, took a different perspective by taking the subject of how liberals leverage a crisis and chaos into their long-term socialist-leaning agenda. We leaned on my unique congressional perspective, having been the chairman of the Oversight and Government Reform Committee and on the Judiciary Committee, among others. I applied those experiences to the rapidly developing crises coming at us on a daily basis. Eric Nelson and David Larabell understood these stories needed to be captured in a book and shared far and wide. I am most grateful they worked together to have me tell these stories and document what was really happening.

Also working on the team from HarperCollins was Hannah Long, whose skillful editing brought clarity and precision to the arguments.

But a book like this, and the tens of thousands of words

flowing together, would have never become reality without the exceptional talents of Jennifer Scott. She has worked with me on a daily basis on all things political since I first approached her about potentially helping me with a run for Congress. I had little to no money for the campaign, but I asked her to join me for lunch so I could tell her about what I was thinking about. I babbled far too long as we sat in a restaurant in Draper, Utah, back in 2007. We have been chatting and exchanging political ideas, thoughts, and perspectives ever since then. I shudder to think about the amount of time and effort she has poured into this journey.

Jennifer is an exceptional person in every way. She cares, loves her family, and loves our country. To her core she believes in freedom and liberty. I could not do what I do without her unparalleled talents. Certainly this book would not have happened had she not worked for months on a daily basis to capture what has been written or said throughout. Thank you, Jennifer. I cannot thank you enough.

Finally, I want to publicly express my love of country. The United States of America is the greatest country on the face of the planet. It has provided more opportunity and prosperity than any other. There is only one America, and she is the best. We should always stand tall for the United States of America. Hmm. Seems like something worth capturing on the pages of a book.

God bless.

INDEX

ABOUT THE AUTHOR

JASON CHAFFETZ is an American politician and Fox News contributor. He was elected as a U.S. representative from Utah in 2008 after spending sixteen years in the local business community. When he left Congress in 2017, he was the chairman of the United States House Committee on Oversight and Government Reform.